THE SCIENTIFIC ENTREPRENEUR

TESTING, FAILING, SUCCEEDING...

TURN EXPERIMENTS INTO EMPIRES – A BLUEPRINT FOR FUTURE BUILDERS

Arham Amit Lalgunkar

BlueRose ONE.com
Stories Matter
NewDelhi • London

BLUEROSE PUBLISHERS
India | U.K.

BlueRose ONE.com
Stories Matter
NewDelhi • London

For permissions requests or inquiries regarding this publication, please contact:

BLUEROSE PUBLISHERS
www.BlueRoseONE.com
info@bluerosepublishers.com
+91 8882 898 898
+4407342408967

ISBN: 978-93-7139-884-8

Cover design: Yash Singhal
Typesetting: Namrata Saini

First Edition: July 2025

DEDICATION PAGE

To the builders who learn by doing.

To the thinkers who experiment relentlessly.

And to everyone brave enough to fail forward.

Acknowledgements

This book is more than just a personal project—it's a reflection of the collective wisdom, support, and inspiration I've received from the many people and platforms that have shaped my thinking.

I begin by expressing my deepest gratitude to **JSS Private School, Dubai**, my academic home and the foundation of my growth. The values, skills, and mindset I cultivated here have been instrumental in shaping this work. I extend heartfelt thanks to the remarkable educators who have guided me with patience, passion, and purpose. A special mention goes to our Principal, **Ms. Chitra Sharma**, for her visionary leadership and commitment to nurturing future innovators; to our Vice Principal, **Ms. Bindhu Rajiv**, for her tireless encouragement and mentorship; and to our CEO, **Mr. Govindrao Naik**, whose support has created an empowering environment where learning goes beyond the classroom.

To all my teachers, thank you for igniting my curiosity and challenging me to think deeper, question boldly, and pursue knowledge relentlessly. You have shaped not only my academic journey but also my character.

To my parents, **Amit Lalgunkar** and **Aditi Lalgunkar**—your unwavering love, endless sacrifices, and unshakable belief in me have been the bedrock of everything I've achieved. You've taught me the value of discipline, compassion, and courage. Thank you for always encouraging me to dream big and for being my biggest supporters through every step of this journey.

To my little brother, **Arin Lalgunkar**—thank you for always keeping it real. One thing I truly admire about you is how you speak your mind with honesty and clarity. Your straightforward way of expressing things has taught me the value of authenticity and staying true to oneself. You inspire me in ways you may not even realize, and I'm lucky to have you as both a brother and a reminder to always stay grounded.

To my uncle, **Amit Patil**—you have been more than family; you have been a mentor, a guide, and a friend. Whether through deep conversations or casual moments, you always found a way to enrich my knowledge and broaden my perspective. Your insights and encouragement in every aspect of life have played a vital role in the shaping of this book and the mindset behind it. I am forever grateful for your presence and wisdom.

To my late grandfather, **Ashok Patil**—your legacy is forever etched in my heart and mind. Though you are no longer with us, your wisdom continues to guide me. You were a pillar of knowledge in my life, and your influence has been profound. Your writings, once published in esteemed Marathi newspapers, are a testament to your intellect and vision. You passed away on **14th April 2025**, but your light still shines through my work. Thank you for the knowledge you so generously passed down and for the guidance that continues to inspire me. Rest in peace.

A heartfelt thanks to **Vinayak Pawar**, who not only designed the first cover page of my book but also provided guidance on how to format and present it in a more creative and professional way. Your artistic sense and thoughtful suggestions helped bring this vision to life with clarity and flair.

To all my extended **family members**, thank you for your constant love, support, and guidance. Your encouragement has uplifted me in moments of doubt and made this journey meaningful and joyful. Each one of you has contributed to the strength and motivation that brought this project to completion.

This book is also a compilation of the knowledge I've gathered from countless sources—from YouTube videos and educational podcasts to business papers, case studies, and social media content shared by modern educators and entrepreneurs. These platforms have become a digital classroom for me, offering insights on entrepreneurship, financial literacy, and innovative ways to earn and grow wealth in today's world. I am especially thankful to the content creators who generously share their expertise, lessons learned, and real-life experiences online. Your efforts have been a guiding light and a practical toolkit for young learners like me.

To every individual—teachers, parents, mentors, creators, and friends—who contributed, directly or indirectly, to my understanding of the world of business and entrepreneurship, I offer my sincerest thanks. Your influence lives in these pages.

This book would not exist without you.

With heartfelt appreciation,
— Arham Amit Lalgunkar

Trademark Acknowledgment

Foreword

In a world where innovation is both the currency and the catalyst of progress, "The Scientific Entrepreneur" by young high school boy Arham Amit Lalgunkar emerges as a clear guidebook. I often encounter experienced professionals seeking clarity, originality, and purpose in their entrepreneurial journeys. This book acts as a SOP, with clarity, originality, and purpose, seamlessly woven into the pages written by a Grade 11 student.

Arham's work defies age-related expectations and offers a mature perspective that bridges the gap between scientific inquiry and entrepreneurial ambition. He does not merely write about entrepreneurship; he redefines it, emphasising analytical thinking, sustained curiosity, and a commitment to learning from failure. These are not just admirable qualities; they are essential attributes of enduring leadership.

Reading this book, I was impressed by Arham's skill in turning complex ideas into accessible insights while upholding intellectual rigour. His views on mentorship, innovation culture, and personal growth show a level of understanding that most only gain after years of experience.

I believe The Scientific Entrepreneur will serve both as a beacon and a blueprint for aspiring changemakers. It reminds us that age is no barrier to insight and that the future of leadership lies in those who combine vision with values.

Congratulations, Arham. You have not only written a book, you've launched an idea whose time has come.

Govinda Rao Naik
CEO
JSS Institutions, Dubai

Foreword

It is with immense pride and admiration that I present this foreword to **The Scientific Entrepreneur**, a remarkable work authored by **Arham Amit Lalgunkar** of **Grade 11B**. As an educator, few moments are as fulfilling as witnessing a young individual rise beyond conventional expectations to contribute meaningfully to the intellectual and creative landscape. Arham has done just that — crafting a book that is not only thought-provoking, but also deeply relevant to the evolving world of innovation and enterprise.

In **The Scientific Entrepreneur**, Arham challenges us to rethink what it means to be an entrepreneur in the 21st century. Rather than being driven by mere ambition or superficial success, he advocates for a mindset rooted in curiosity, experimentation, and thoughtful reflection — the very traits that define a true scientist. This synthesis of entrepreneurial drive and scientific thinking presents a compelling blueprint for the next generation of changemakers.

What makes this book truly inspiring is the clarity of vision and maturity of thought Arham brings to his writing. He explores themes such as resilience, learning from failure, and the role of digital mentorship with insight and depth well beyond his years. It is rare to see such intellectual engagement and disciplined execution in a student so young.

I am confident that **The Scientific Entrepreneur** will not only resonate with aspiring entrepreneurs and educators alike but will also inspire young minds everywhere to approach challenges with curiosity, courage, and a spirit of inquiry.

Congratulations, Arham, on this outstanding accomplishment. The future belongs to thinkers like you.

Regards
Chitra Sharma Principal
JSS Private School Dubai

Foreword

It gives me great joy and pride to write this foreword for The Scientific Entrepreneur, a compelling and insightful work by one of our brightest young minds, Arham Amit Lalgunkar of Grade 11B. As Vice Principal, I have had the privilege of observing Arham's academic journey, and this book stands as a testament to his curiosity, determination, and deeply reflective nature.

The Scientific Entrepreneur is more than a student's exploration of innovation—it is a mature and articulate reflection on what it means to pursue meaningful change in today's complex world. Arham's approach is refreshingly thoughtful. He invites us to view entrepreneurship not just as a business venture, but as a disciplined practice of inquiry, experimentation, and ethical action—hallmarks of a scientific mindset.

What impresses me most is Arham's ability to draw connections between personal development and broader societal impact. His treatment of topics like resilience, digital mentorship, and the power of failure is handled with both depth and sincerity, providing valuable insights for learners and educators alike.

This book is a proud milestone—not just for Arham, but for all of us who believe in nurturing young thinkers who dare to ask questions and build solutions. I am confident that The Scientific Entrepreneur will ignite curiosity and inspire initiative in everyone who reads it.

Well done, Arham. Your voice matters—and it's only just begun to be heard.

Bindhu Rajiv Vice Principal
JSS Private School Dubai

Foreword

There are moments in every family, every school, and every community when a young voice rises—not with noise, but with purpose. The Scientific Entrepreneur is one such voice, and it belongs to Arham, a remarkable 16-year-old student of JSS Private School, Dubai.

While many of his peers are still trying to discover what interests them, Arham found his passion early on: a fascination with how ideas evolve into successful businesses and how visionaries impact the world through their work. What truly distinguishes him is not just his curiosity but also his commitment. Over the past two and a half years, amidst schoolwork and events, he has read, listened, reflected, and researched tirelessly. Podcasts became his classrooms, articles served as his teachers, and books acted like mentors. What came out of this journey is this very book—a thoughtful collection of the principles, qualities, and mindsets that underpin successful entrepreneurs.

"The Scientific Entrepreneur" is not just a book; it's evidence that age doesn't limit one's insight. It shows that discipline, passion, and a thirst for knowledge can lead to meaningful contributions—even before reaching adulthood. Arham reminds us that the next generation of thinkers and doers is already here, shaping the future with fresh perspectives and focused minds.

Until now, Arham has been known as a student, a son, a nephew. With the launch of this book, he becomes something more—a published author, a thought leader in the making, and a young man whose journey will inspire many.

We are proud to be known as Arham's family, friends, and teachers. The world is getting to know him now—and this is just the beginning.

— **Amit Patil**
(On behalf of all who proudly stand behind Arham)

Foreword

Every once in a while, a voice emerges that defies expectations—not just because of what it says, but because of who is saying it. Arham Lalgunkar is one of those voices. At just sixteen years old, Arham has written a book that speaks with more clarity, insight, and purpose than many seasoned professionals twice his age. Even more impressively, he began this journey at fourteen, not waiting for permission or the "right time," but instead letting curiosity and ambition lead the way.

The Scientific Entrepreneur: Testing, Failing, Succeeding… is not a textbook. It's a testament. A testament to the idea that age is no barrier to innovation, that failure is not the opposite of success but part of the process, and that entrepreneurship isn't just about building businesses—it's about building yourself.

In these pages, Arham offers a refreshing lens on the entrepreneurial mindset. He approaches it like a scientist—experimenting, learning from failure, analyzing outcomes—and yet never loses the heart and hustle that drive great entrepreneurs. His insights are both thoughtful and practical, drawn from real attempts, real setbacks, and real growth.

What makes this book remarkable is not just the wisdom it shares, but the reminder it offers to all of us—young or old—that boldness, curiosity, and resilience are timeless traits. Arham doesn't just tell us how to think like an entrepreneur; he shows us, through his own evolving journey.

To the reader: this is more than a guidebook. It's a spark. Let it ignite your own journey, and remind you that the future doesn't belong to those who wait—it belongs to those, like Arham, who dare to begin.

- Vismay Walle

Table of Contents

INTRODUCTION

A New Kind of Entrepreneur

The world is no longer kind to blind optimism. In an era defined by rapid disruption, relentless competition, and increasing complexity, the entrepreneurs who succeed aren't the ones who shout the loudest, raise the most capital, or hustle until burnout.

They're the ones who think like scientists.

This book is for a new kind of builder—one who questions assumptions, runs experiments instead of blindly executing plans, and views failure not as defeat but as data. In this mindset, every setback is a signal, every obstacle is an opportunity to test, and every win is the result of deliberate, evidence-based learning.

The Scientific Entrepreneur offers a framework built on the core principles of curiosity, iteration, measurement, and resilience. You'll meet entrepreneurs and companies that pivoted based on hypotheses, grew through disciplined feedback loops, and adapted using metrics—not just momentum. And more importantly, you'll learn how to integrate those same tools and mental models into your own work, regardless of what you're building.

But let me be clear—this is not a book of abstract theory.

This is a **field manual**.

Each chapter is designed to give you practical strategies to experiment more effectively, think more critically, and adapt more intelligently. The goal isn't to make you reckless. It's to make you rigorous. To empower you to build not from guesswork, but from grounded insights.

To make you dangerous—in the best way.

Whether you're launching your first startup, scaling your fifth, or simply trying to approach life and work with greater clarity, my hope is that this book becomes a companion for your journey. One that encourages you to build with less ego and more evidence. With fewer assumptions and more understanding. With a confidence rooted not in hype—but in the quiet certainty of someone who knows how to learn, test, and grow.

A Note on the Origins of This Book

This book is also a **compilation of knowledge** gathered across years of exploration—from insightful **YouTube videos**, deep-dive **business papers**, **online courses**, and the content generously shared by creators and entrepreneurs on **social media platforms**. These digital mentors offered a modern education in entrepreneurship, finance, and personal growth. Their lessons have been absorbed, tested, applied, and are now embedded into the pages that follow.

In many ways, this is not just my book.

It is a reflection of a larger learning community—online and offline—that made these ideas accessible, real, and transformative.

Because in the end, real success doesn't lie in a single outcome.

It lives in the **process**.

The process of becoming someone who experiments relentlessly, learns continuously, and builds fearlessly.

Let's begin.

CHAPTER 1

The Mindset Shift – From Dreamer to Designer

Most people who start a business are fueled by passion. They're driven by a powerful idea, a product they believe the world needs, or a vision of financial independence. That passion is valuable—it's the spark that starts the fire.

But fire without direction can be dangerous.

The Risk of Passion Without Process

Passion can blind you to reality. It can make you ignore market signals, dismiss critical feedback, and pour time and money into something untested—something that feels right but may not work.

That's how businesses fail before they truly begin.

The mindset shift we're talking about in this book is simple but profound:

Don't build a business like a dreamer. Build it like a scientist.

This means replacing assumptions with observations, replacing intuition with inquiry, and replacing belief with testing. It doesn't mean killing your passion—but channeling it through a process that increases your odds of real success.

Let's explore what that looks like.

The Traditional Mindset: Build It and Hope

We've all seen the Hollywood version of entrepreneurship: the visionary who has an "aha" moment, quits their job, maxes out their credit cards, builds something brilliant, and strikes it big.

This narrative is romantic—but it's misleading.

In the real world, 90% of startups fail. And one of the most common reasons? Building something no one actually wants.

The traditional mindset sounds like this:

- "This product is amazing. People will definitely buy it."
- "There's nothing like this out there, so I have no competition."
- "If I build it just right, the market will come to me."

These beliefs lead people to spend months—even years—building a perfect version of something… only to discover that the market doesn't care.

That's not entrepreneurship. That's wishful thinking.

The Scientific Mindset: Test, Measure, Adapt

The scientific entrepreneur approaches things differently. Just like a scientist in a lab, they:

- Observe the environment for patterns, pain points, and unmet needs.
- Form a hypothesis about what kind of solution might work.
- Design an experiment—usually a minimum viable product (MVP) or low-cost test.
- Collect data based on real customer behavior.
- Analyze the results to determine what to change, keep, or eliminate.
- Iterate and re-test, continually learning and improving.

This doesn't eliminate risk, but it makes failure useful.

Mindset Example: Thomas Edison and the Light Bulb

When Thomas Edison was asked how it felt to fail 1,000 times before inventing the light bulb, he replied:

"I have not failed. I've just found 1,000 ways that won't work."

That's the scientific mindset in action. Every failed attempt was a data point. Each one narrowed the path toward a working solution. Entrepreneurs should treat their products the same way—not as binary successes or failures, but as evolving experiments.

Case Study: Dropbox's Video MVP

When Dropbox was first starting out, the founders could have spent months building the full product. Instead, they created a short explainer video that demonstrated how the product would work—if it existed.

The video gained thousands of sign-ups, validating that there was strong demand before a single line of production code was written.

That's science: test the hypothesis, observe the reaction, measure demand.

Why This Mindset Matters So Much

- **You'll Save Time and Money:** Experiments are cheaper than finished products.
- **You'll Learn Faster:** Every test brings real-world feedback.
- **You'll Become Resilient:** Failure doesn't feel like an identity crisis—it's part of the process.
- **You'll Make Smarter Decisions:** You're not guessing—you're guided by data.

Most importantly, you'll stop fearing failure and start using it.

From Artist to Engineer

This mindset shift isn't about killing creativity. It's about channeling it.

Think of your role not as an artist crafting a masterpiece, but as an engineer building a bridge. It doesn't matter how "beautiful" the bridge is if it collapses under weight. The job is to make it stand—then make it elegant.

Start with what works. Then make it better.

Action Steps to Start Thinking Scientifically

Here are some prompts to help shift into the scientific mindset:

- List 3 assumptions you're making about your idea. Which ones could be false?
- Design a mini experiment that tests one of those assumptions within a week.
- Talk to 5 people who might use your product. What do they complain about regularly?
- Define success metrics. What data will tell you if your experiment is working?
- Embrace failure. Ask yourself, "What would I learn if this fails?"

You don't need to have all the answers now. You just need the courage to start testing.

Closing Thought: Curiosity Over Certainty

Certainty kills innovation. Curiosity fuels it.

The scientific entrepreneur stays curious. They don't get stuck on being right—they're obsessed with getting it right. And that makes all the difference.

In the chapters ahead, we'll dive deeper into each element of this scientific approach—how to observe, test, measure, and evolve your business with purpose and precision.

But it all starts here: with the mindset.

Chapter 1: The Mindset Shift — From Dreamer to Designer

- How do you stay grounded when pursuing ambitious goals?
- What mental shifts helped you move from ideas to actionable steps?
- How do you deal with setbacks that challenge your initial vision?
- Can you describe how experimentation plays a role in your work?

CHAPTER 2

Observation and Hypothesis — Seeing What Others Miss

> *"The first principle is that you must not fool yourself—and you are the easiest person to fool."* — *Richard Feynman*

In science, everything begins with observation. Before a scientist forms a hypothesis or runs an experiment, they look. They study the world, gather data, and notice patterns—especially the ones others ignore.

Entrepreneurship works the same way.

Too many businesses are built on assumptions. But real opportunities lie in painfully obvious problems that no one has truly solved—or even noticed. If Chapter 1 was about shifting your mindset from dreamer to designer, this chapter is about refining your lens. It's about cultivating your ability to observe the world deeply and draw insight from what others overlook. The best entrepreneurs don't just invent solutions. They observe problems with clarity, curiosity, and humility.

The Entrepreneur's First Tool: Clear Observation

Observation is the foundation of all scientific thought—and it should be the foundation of your business as well. It means noticing what's *really* happening, not what you *hope* is happening. It means studying people and systems in the wild. What do they complain about? What do they tolerate but clearly dislike? Where are they inventing workarounds or wasting time?

In entrepreneurship, observation isn't passive—it's a deliberate practice. You're not waiting for inspiration; you're searching for friction.

Start paying attention to the everyday workarounds people create. Notice when someone says, "It's not ideal, but we've found a way to make it work." That's opportunity disguised as compromise. Entrepreneurs who learn to notice these compromises become the ones who solve them—and build companies around those solutions

Case Study: Uber and the Power of Frustration

The founders of Uber didn't start by saying, "Let's build a global ride-hailing app." They started with a frustrating experience—trying to find a taxi in Paris on a rainy night. That simple pain point—one that millions experienced every day—was the origin of a multibillion-dollar company.

They observed three key frustrations:

- Unreliable access to taxis
- No transparency on when or whether a ride would arrive
- Inconsistent and unpredictable pricing

From that starting point, they asked a powerful question: What if getting a ride was as easy as pushing a button on your phone?

That question didn't emerge from a whiteboard session or a product brainstorm. It came from watching the world closely and asking why it didn't work better.

How to Train Your Observational Muscles

Like any scientific skill, observation can be improved with practice. Here are a few methods to enhance your ability to see opportunity:

1. Be Where the Problems Are

Immerse yourself in the environment of your target customers. If you're building for restaurant owners, spend time in busy kitchens. If you're designing for freelancers, talk to them between projects. Don't rely on secondhand insights. Experience the chaos, the tension, and the hacks people use to survive.

When Steve Jobs wanted to reinvent the personal computer, he didn't just study technology—he observed how people interacted with it. That empathy fueled the intuitive simplicity of the Mac.

2. Listen Without Selling

When you talk to potential customers, silence your inner salesperson. Ask open-ended questions like:

- "What's the most frustrating part of your day?"
- "Where do you feel you waste the most time or money?"
- "What's something you wish existed but can't find?"

Your job is to understand pain—not pitch a solution. Focus on how people describe their challenges. The exact language they use will become gold when you eventually build and market your product.

3. Track Patterns, Not Outliers

If one person has a problem, it might be unique. But if ten people describe the same pain in different words, you've found a pattern—and likely a market. Start a *Problem Journal*. Write down every complaint, inefficiency, or workaround you encounter. Revisit your notes weekly to look for common threads.

Observation is a discipline. When practiced regularly, it changes how you see the world—and makes you dangerous in the best possible way.

From Observation to Hypothesis: The Scientific Shift

Once you've gathered real-world insights, it's time to form a hypothesis—a testable guess about a solution. This is where the magic of science meets the art of entrepreneurship.

In science, a hypothesis isn't a belief. It's a temporary assumption you're willing to test. In business, a good hypothesis might sound like:

> "If we create [this feature], then [these people] will [take this specific action]."

Or…

> "If we offer [this service], then [target customers] will pay [a certain amount] to solve [a specific problem]."

A hypothesis is the bridge between insight and action.

Example: Airbnb's Origin Hypothesis

- **Observation**: Hotels are overpriced and overbooked during conferences.
- **Hypothesis**: Attendees might pay to sleep in someone's spare bedroom during events.

Instead of building a full platform, the Airbnb founders tested their idea by renting out their own apartment and building a simple landing page. The test succeeded—and gave them the confidence to build further.

They didn't start with code. They started with an insight and a minimal test.

What Makes a Good Hypothesis?

A strong hypothesis has three qualities:

1. **Specific** — You can define exactly what you're testing.

2. **Testable** — You can run a real experiment and gather data.
3. **Relevant** — It addresses a real, observed pain point.

Compare these:

- ❌ "People want better productivity tools." (Vague)
- ✅ "If we help freelancers track tasks and time in one place, they'll save 3 hours a week and pay $10/month." (Specific and testable)

When your hypothesis is clear, testing becomes simple. You'll know exactly what to build, who to show it to, and what to measure.

Why This Process Is So Often Skipped

Inexperienced entrepreneurs skip observation and hypothesis formation because it's slow. They're in a rush to build. They want to feel progress. But skipping this step is like pouring concrete before measuring the foundation.

Without clear insights and testable assumptions, you risk building the wrong thing incredibly well. You may spend months perfecting a product that solves a non-existent problem.

This is why many founders say, "We just need better marketing." But the real issue isn't awareness—it's relevance. No amount of advertising can sell a solution no one needs.

The Problem-First Principle

Before you build anything, complete this sentence:

> "I believe that [this group of people] struggles with [this clear, specific problem], and that [my idea] might help them solve it."

If you can't write this down confidently, you're not ready to build yet.

Every successful product begins with this clarity. It's your compass in the chaos of entrepreneurship.

Case Study: Dropbox's MVP That Wasn't a Product

When Dropbox first explored launching a file-syncing service, the founders didn't spend months building complex infrastructure. Instead, they recorded a **two-minute explainer video** demonstrating how the product *would* work—if it existed.

That video was shared with early adopters. Thousands signed up to the waitlist. The message was clear: people *wanted* what Dropbox planned to offer.

That's a scientific test. No guesswork. Just clear observation, a sharp hypothesis, and rapid validation.

Action Steps: Applying Observation and Hypothesis Today

Let's make this real for you.

Step 1: Interview 5 Real People

Talk to people who represent your target audience. Don't mention your idea. Just ask about their problems, inefficiencies, and frustrations. Let them speak freely.

Step 2: Write Down 3 Repeated Problems

From your interviews, isolate three pain points that came up repeatedly. These are the raw ingredients for your hypothesis.

Step 3: Form One Hypothesis

Craft a specific, testable assumption using this structure:

"If we [do X], then [Y] will happen for [Z group]."

Example:

"If we allow students to reserve group study rooms online, they'll use the system weekly and reduce campus bottlenecks."

Step 4: Sketch a Mini Experiment

Design a small test to validate your hypothesis. This could be:

- A landing page with a call to action
- A survey gauging interest
- A clickable prototype
- A conversation with prospective users showing a concept

Keep it simple. Remember: you're not trying to *win*, you're trying to *learn*.

Why Observation and Hypothesis Are the Heart of Innovation

Ideas are everywhere. But *validated* ideas are rare. That's what sets scientific entrepreneurs apart. They don't fall in love with ideas—they fall in love with the process of learning what works.

The best founders are *part detective, part scientist*. They watch the world carefully. They test ideas methodically. And when they're wrong, they adapt rather than defend their ego.

In other words, they don't guess. They discover.

Closing Thought: See Before You Solve

In the rush to build, many founders forget the first step: *look carefully*. Your greatest asset is not your idea—it's your understanding of the problem.

In the next chapter, we'll explore how to take your observations and hypotheses and design minimum viable experiments—ones that test your assumptions without wasting time, money, or momentum.

But for now, commit to seeing clearly. Because the truth is this:

> Entrepreneurs who observe with discipline earn the right to invent with confidence.

Chapter 2: Observation and Hypothesis — Seeing What Others Miss

- What techniques do you use to notice overlooked opportunities?
- How do you form testable hypotheses from vague observations?
- Can you share how observation changed your approach to a problem?
- How do you balance data gathering with intuition during exploration?

CHAPTER 3

Minimum Viable Experiments – Test Before You Build

> *"The only way to win is to learn faster than anyone else."*
> *— Eric Ries, The Lean Startup*

Introduction: The Trap of Premature Building

Entrepreneurs are naturally inclined to create. It's in our DNA to envision a solution and immediately want to bring it to life. We sketch prototypes, write code, commission designs, or file patents—all before confirming whether anyone even wants what we're offering.

In science, ideas aren't launched—they're tested. Every hypothesis is subject to scrutiny, doubt, and experimentation. Only after surviving rigorous trials does a theory earn its place. Entrepreneurs should adopt the same mindset.

This is where the **Minimum Viable Experiment (MVE)** becomes invaluable. It's not a diluted version of your product. It's the tool that tells you whether the problem you observed is real, whether your hypothesis holds weight, and whether your idea deserves to live.

If Chapter 2 taught you to see like a scientist, Chapter 3 will teach you to act like one—by building small, testing early, and learning fast.

What is a Minimum Viable Experiment?

A **Minimum Viable Experiment** is the smallest, cheapest, and fastest way to validate a specific assumption about your business idea. It's not a product, it's a probe. It gathers data, not revenue. It minimizes risk, not features.

Think of it as a **learning loop**. The MVE helps you:

- Test whether your solution is **desirable**.
- Get **real user feedback** before building.
- Make clear decisions—**pivot, persevere, or pause**.

You're not making something for users to love just yet. You're creating something for them to react to—positively, negatively, or indifferently.

> **Key Principle**: *Your job at this stage is not to sell—it's to learn.*

Why Entrepreneurs Build Too Much

Entrepreneurs love building because it feels productive and rewarding. But here's the hard truth: building without testing is the fastest way to waste your time, money, and momentum.

You can spend months crafting a polished product—only to discover that:

- No one wants it.
- They don't understand it.
- They aren't willing to pay for it.
- Or someone else already does it better.

Many founders fall into this trap and justify it with statements like:

> "We just need better marketing."
>
> "Users don't get it yet."
>
> "It's early days—they'll come."

But in reality, they skipped the learning phase. They built a solution before validating the problem.

> **Scientific entrepreneurs don't fall in love with their ideas. They fall in love with learning whether the idea works.**

Case Studies: Experiments that Changed the Game

✅ Dropbox – The Explainer Video

Drew Houston's team didn't start by building a complex syncing engine. Instead, they created a 3-minute video that *pretended* Dropbox existed. It visually demonstrated the product's core value.

The result? Over 75,000 people signed up for the beta waiting list overnight.

> **Lesson**: Don't build it. *Show* it.

✅ Buffer – The Landing Page Test

The Buffer team wanted to know if people would pay for a social media scheduling tool. So they built a simple landing page with pricing tiers. When users clicked, they saw: "We're not ready yet—sign up to be notified."

Thousands did.

> **Lesson**: Measure intent before writing code.

✅ Zappos – The Manual Storefront

Before launching a full-scale online shoe retailer, Nick Swinmurn tested his hypothesis by photographing shoes from local stores and uploading them to a basic website. When someone ordered, he went to the store, bought the shoes, and shipped them manually.

It wasn't scalable—but it was enough to prove the demand.

> **Lesson**: Use *people*, not platforms, to test delivery.

☑ Food on the Table – The Concierge MVP

Instead of building an app to help families plan meals and shop smarter, the founder started by doing it manually—calling families, checking grocery store deals, and assembling meal plans by hand.

Once enough people paid for that service, he knew it was worth automating.

Lesson: Deliver the value by hand first. Scale later.

How to Design a Minimum Viable Experiment

Here's a step-by-step guide to crafting your own MVE:

Step 1: Define the Hypothesis

Start by articulating your hypothesis clearly:

- "If we offer [X], then [Y] will happen."
- "We believe [specific user] has [specific problem] and will [specific action] if we present [our solution]."

Example:

"Freelancers will pay $10/month for a simple app to track time and send invoices."

Step 2: Choose a Focused Assumption to Test

You can't test everything at once. Identify the *riskiest* or *most foundational* assumption first.

Examples:

- Do people *want* this?
- Will they *pay* for it?
- Do they *understand* it?
- Is the problem *painful enough*?

Step 3: Select the Right Test Format

Choose the leanest format that will give you evidence:

What You Want to Learn	Possible MVE Format
Do people want it?	Landing page + ad traffic
Will they pay?	Offer pre-orders or pricing test
Do they understand it?	Mockup + explanation session
Can you deliver value manually?	Concierge test (do it yourself)
Will they engage?	Email sequence, prototype, or demo

Step 4: Set Success Metrics

Before launching the experiment, define what counts as success. This keeps you honest.

Example:

"If 30 out of 100 visitors click 'Sign Up,' we proceed. If fewer than 10 do, we pause and reevaluate."

Step 5: Run Fast, Learn Hard

Launch your MVE within 7–10 days. Don't overthink it. Don't overbuild.

Then look at:

- Engagement data (clicks, signups)
- Feedback from users
- Conversion or payment indicators
- Comments or qualitative insights

> **Reminder**: If the data says "no one cares," that's a win—you've just saved months of wasted effort.

Overcoming Psychological Barriers

Many entrepreneurs resist the idea of "minimum." It can feel like cheating or settling. But in the scientific mindset, "minimum" is a virtue. It forces clarity. It prioritizes learning over polish.

> "If you're not embarrassed by the first version of your product, you've launched too late."
>
> — Reid Hoffman, LinkedIn Founder

You're not cutting corners. You're cutting *waste*.

Common MVE Mistakes to Avoid

Let's bulletproof your approach. Watch out for these traps:

- ✖ **Overbuilding**: A perfect logo or app won't save a flawed idea.
- ✖ **Vague goals**: Always define what success looks like ahead of time.
- ✖ **Testing too much**: One variable at a time. Clarity > complexity.
- ✖ **Ignoring feedback**: When users are confused or uninterested—pay attention.
- ✖ **Confirmation bias**: Don't interpret weak signals as validation. Be brutally honest with yourself.

Thought Exercise: Design Your First MVE

Let's make this real. Fill in the blanks:

> I believe that [target customer] has [clear problem] and that [my idea] can help them solve it.
>
> I will test this by [experiment format] and it will be successful if [success metric].

Example:

> I believe that remote developers struggle with time tracking and that a simple mobile timer can help them.

> I'll create a landing page and run $50 of Facebook ads.
>
> If 10% or more click and 5% leave their email, I'll move forward.

Now—it's your turn.

Action Steps for This Week

☑ Write down 1–2 hypotheses about your idea.

☑ Design a small, focused experiment (landing page, mockup, video, or manual delivery).

☑ Define a clear success metric.

☑ Launch within 7 days.

☑ Review the results and decide: **pivot, persevere, or pause**.

Closing Thought: Build to Learn, Not Just to Launch

The startup graveyard is filled with beautiful products that no one needed. But scientific entrepreneurs survive and thrive because they test their way forward.

They don't just build for the sake of launching. They build *to learn.*

A Minimum Viable Experiment gives you data, insight, and momentum. It lets you take smart steps—not blind leaps.

> So ask yourself: What's the smallest possible test that could teach me the most important thing?

Start there.

Chapter 3: Minimum Viable Experiments — Test Before You Build

- How do you decide what the smallest experiment should be?
- What's your process for testing ideas with limited resources?
- Can you describe a time when a small test changed your strategy?
- How do you interpret early experiment results without overreacting?

CHAPTER 4

Failure Is Data – Why Losing Can Be a Win

> *"I have not failed. I've just found 10,000 ways that won't work." — Thomas Edison*

Failure. The very word can tighten your chest, ignite anxiety, and summon waves of doubt. Most people avoid failure like the plague. In school, it's a red mark. In society, it's a stain. In business, it feels like the loss of credibility—public proof that you didn't have what it takes.

But scientific entrepreneurs see failure differently.

They don't fear it.

They don't run from it.

They don't sugarcoat it.

They analyze it.

Because failure isn't the opposite of success. It's the lab coat of progress. It's an essential input to the learning machine. Like a negative test result in a lab, failure clarifies what doesn't work—so you can get closer to what does.

Rethinking Failure: From Emotion to Experiment

Traditional culture treats failure as a verdict. You tried, you lost, end of story. But this emotional view misses the point.

Entrepreneurs operating from a scientific mindset don't treat failure as an emotional blow. They see it as data.

Failure is feedback.

Failure is signal.

Failure is evidence.

When seen correctly, it tells you where to go next.

- Scientific entrepreneurs ask:
- What was our assumption?
- What result did we expect?
- What actually happened?
- What can we now test better?

The goal is never to avoid being wrong—it's to **learn** as fast and as accurately as possible.

Failure in Science vs. Business

In science, a failed experiment is not a personal defeat. It's a step toward understanding reality. If your hypothesis doesn't match the data, you revise the hypothesis—not your self-worth.

But in business, we often confuse identity with outcomes. A failed product can feel like a failed self.

That confusion is dangerous.

The market isn't judging your morality or character. It's reacting to your offer. Your product didn't convert? That's not a reflection of you. It's a data point on what users value, understand, or want to pay for.

A scientific entrepreneur knows: the market isn't your mom. It won't lie to protect your feelings.

The Cost of Avoiding Failure

Avoiding failure may feel safe. But it's deadly for innovation.

It looks like this:

- Spending a year perfecting a product no one asked for.
- Refusing to show prototypes until they're "ready."
- Ignoring complaints because they're uncomfortable.
- Writing off negative feedback as "haters."

This mindset protects ego, not progress.

The truth? The longer you hide from failure, the more expensive it becomes. A failed landing page is cheap. A failed company, built on untested assumptions, is not.

Every month you delay learning is a month you burn resources.

Your real job is not to build impressive things. It's to uncover truth—fast, cheap, and clearly.

Three Types of Failure (And How to Use Each One)

Let's break down failure like a scientist dissects results.

✖ Type 1: Unclear Failure

You launch something… and it flops. But you're not sure why. There was no clear hypothesis, no data tracking, no user feedback.

This is the worst kind of failure: expensive and vague.

Fix: Always set clear learning goals before you launch. Know what you're testing. Track the right behaviors. Get both quantitative and qualitative feedback.

✖ Type 2: Ego-Protected Failure

The data says one thing, but you spin it to match your hope. You tell yourself:

- "It was just the wrong time."
- "They didn't understand it."
- "Our audience wasn't ready."

This is emotional self-defense disguised as analysis.

Fix: Be ruthlessly honest. Data doesn't lie—but you can. Get a second pair of eyes on the metrics if needed. Make decisions from evidence, not ego.

✅ Type 3: Productive Failure

You set a clear test. The result was negative. But now you know why. You learn. You adapt.

This is golden. Celebrate this kind of failure. It's the cornerstone of iteration.

Fix: Document the lesson. Share it with your team. Use it to sharpen your next hypothesis.

Case Study: Instagram's Failure Led to Focus

Instagram began as a bloated check-in app called Burbn. It had messaging, location tagging, gamification—none of it really stuck. The founders watched the usage data. Most features bombed.

Except one: photo sharing.

Rather than doubling down on a failing bundle of features, they cut everything but the photo tool and rebranded.

The result? Instagram as we know it.

Their success wasn't despite failure—it was born from it.

How to Analyze a Failed Experiment

Let's say your Minimum Viable Experiment (MVE) flopped. No signups. No sales. No interest. What now?

Use this framework:

1. **Detach emotionally** – This is a test, not a tattoo. It doesn't define you.
2. **Review your hypothesis** – Was it specific and falsifiable?
3. **Audit your inputs** – Did enough people see the experiment? Were they the right people?
4. **Observe behavior** – Where did people drop off? Did they click? Scroll? Engage?
5. **Collect direct feedback** – Use surveys, interviews, or session replays to find confusion points.
6. **Extract insights** – What assumption did the test disprove? What can you improve?
7. **Retest smartly** – Adjust one key variable and run the next experiment quickly.

Don't fear the retest. Each iteration is smarter than the last.

Real-Life Example: Zappos' Humble Start

Nick Swinmurn, founder of Zappos, wanted to test if people would buy shoes online. Instead of building inventory or warehouses, he went to local stores, photographed shoes, and posted them online.

When someone bought a pair, he'd return to the store, purchase the shoes, and ship them manually.

It was clunky, inefficient, and unscalable.

But it was a brilliant experiment.

People bought shoes. Assumption validated. Zappos was born.

Had he waited to build a full e-commerce platform, he may have spent millions learning the same lesson.

Your New Goal: Fast, Cheap, Useful Failure

The best entrepreneurs don't avoid failure. They optimize for it. Specifically, they aim for:

- **Fast failure**: Learn early before investing deeply.
- **Cheap failure**: Use simple tests, not expensive campaigns.
- **Useful failure**: Design tests that answer clear questions.

This approach is part of what Nassim Taleb calls being *antifragile*—systems that improve through stress.

Your startup should be the same. Every failure should strengthen your understanding, your offering, and your execution.

The Psychology of Failure: Burning the Shame

Shame is failure's most dangerous companion. It tells you that your failure is a reflection of your identity.

Scientific entrepreneurs kill shame with structure. They don't say, "I failed." They say, "That test failed."

They separate self from outcome. They keep the signal and discard the shame.

That shift gives them freedom—freedom to experiment, iterate, and grow.

Action Steps: Transform Failure into Fuel

1. List Your Last 3 Failures
2. Whether business, product, pitch, or partnership—identify what didn't work.
3. Extract the Assumptions
4. What belief did each failure disprove?
5. Analyze the Data
6. Were you missing feedback, targeting the wrong audience, or miscommunicating value?

7. Design One New Test
8. Take one insight and craft a new MVE. Run it within 7 days.
9. Track and Share the Learning
10. Capture what happens. Share the lesson with your team or community.

This will change how you see failure. It becomes fuel—not friction.

Closing Thought: Failure Is the Feedback Loop of the Future

You won't build a breakthrough company by getting everything right the first time.

You'll build it by getting the important things right over time—through constant learning.

Failure is not a red light. It's a flashlight. It shines on what needs to change, what you must improve, and where the truth lies.

So test bravely. Fail intelligently. Learn relentlessly.

Because the entrepreneurs who ultimately succeed are not those who dodge every fall—but those who stand up faster, smarter, and clearer every single time.

🧪 Chapter 4 — The Feedback Loop of Failure

Choose one:

Identify a recent failure. Reframe it in writing as a data point, not a defeat. What experiment does it suggest?

Ask 3 customers or users: "What confused you most about what I offer?" Turn their answers into a next-step hypothesis.

Chapter 4: Failure Is Data — Why Losing Can Be a Win

- How do you separate emotional response from learning when things fail?

- What methods help you extract useful feedback from failures?
- Can you share an example where a failure led to a better approach?
- How do you encourage a culture that views failure as learning?

CHAPTER 5

The Iteration Cycle – Build, Measure, Learn, Repeat

> *"Innovation is not about having the best idea. It's about relentlessly testing and refining until it works." — Anonymous startup founder*

Entrepreneurs often imagine success as a straight path. You have a great idea, you build it, you launch it—and boom, success.

But the reality, for those who've lived it, is far more circular than linear.

The real trajectory of successful startups looks more like this:

Build, fail, adjust. Test, learn, tweak. Try again. Then again. Then again.

It's the rhythm of iteration.

This chapter explores the most powerful pattern in the scientific entrepreneur's playbook: **the Build–Measure–Learn cycle.** You'll learn how to run tight loops of experimentation, how to extract learning from every output, and how to make smarter decisions with every turn of the wheel.

Why Iteration Beats Perfection

Perfectionism kills startups. Not because perfect is bad—but because it's slow, expensive, and usually wrong.

The iterative mindset flips the equation. Instead of trying to be right, you try to **learn fast.** You accept that you won't get it right on the first try—and that's fine. Your job is to minimize the cost of being wrong and maximize the value of what you learn next.

In science, experiments are designed to be run, reviewed, and refined. That's how discoveries are made.

In entrepreneurship, iteration works the same way.

Instead of a launch-and-pray approach, the scientific entrepreneur launches, measures, analyzes—and improves.

The Origin of the Loop: Build – Measure – Learn

Eric Ries popularized the *Build–Measure–Learn* loop in *The Lean Startup*. But this isn't just a catchy phrase. It's a precise workflow that mirrors the scientific method in business.

Let's break it down:

1. Build – Create a testable version of your idea

This isn't "build the full product." It means create the **minimum viable artifact** needed to run a test.

- A landing page
- A prototype
- A service offered manually
- A video simulation
- A pricing test

Whatever form it takes, it must represent a real hypothesis in action.

2. Measure – Collect meaningful data from real users

Here, vanity metrics are your enemy. You don't want just traffic, likes, or shares. You want signals tied to **action**:

- Click-through rates

- Conversion rates
- Time spent
- Drop-off points
- User feedback and objections

Measurement is about observation. And great observers notice both what is there—and what is missing.

3. Learn – Make sense of what happened

Once you've measured outcomes, you analyze them through the lens of your hypothesis. You ask:

- What did we expect to happen?
- What actually happened?
- What does that tell us?
- What should we change?

The loop isn't complete until you've extracted **real learning**. And that learning drives the next build.

The Power of Tight Feedback Loops

Speed matters. Not because rushing is good—but because long delays between action and feedback kill momentum and mislead judgment.

In a startup, long feedback loops look like this:

- Building a full product for 6 months
- Launching to silence
- Then wondering what went wrong

That's a catastrophic iteration cycle. You learn one thing every six months.

Now compare that to a tight loop:

- You launch a landing page on Monday
- Run ads by Tuesday

- Get 300 visits by Wednesday
- Review analytics Thursday
- Launch version 2 by Friday

That's 5 days per loop. Fifty learnings in a year instead of two.

Speed = More data = Better decisions = Higher odds of success.

Case Study: Superhuman's Onboarding Iterations

Superhuman, the high-speed email client, used relentless iteration to improve their onboarding.

They didn't just build a signup flow. They built, measured, and learned from every click, question, and complaint. Founder Rahul Vohra used one core question to track learning:

> "How disappointed would you be if you could no longer use Superhuman?"

If less than 40% of users said "very disappointed," they didn't move forward. Instead, they studied why—down to the smallest objection—and reworked the product.

This feedback loop drove everything: design, feature priority, and messaging.

The result? A fiercely loyal user base and a product people love before it goes public.

Iteration vs. Pivoting: Know the Difference

A **pivot** is a big directional change—a shift in strategy, target market, or product use.

An **iteration** is a small adjustment—a refinement of wording, layout, features, or positioning.

Here's why this matters:

Don't pivot when you should iterate. Don't iterate when you should pivot.

Think of it like this:

Problem	Solution
Users are interested but not converting	Iterate: test pricing, layout, messaging
No one is engaging at all	Pivot: rethink the core offering or market
Users love the idea but not the delivery	Iterate: improve UX, speed, clarity
Users are confused about the value	Iterate: simplify language, value prop

A smart entrepreneur always starts with iteration. Pivots are based on **patterns** of failed iterations—not single experiments.

The Iteration Playbook: Step-by-Step

Step 1: Identify a Key Assumption

What is one belief you're holding that affects your product or strategy?

Example:

- People will pay $20/month for my tool
- Professionals want video tutorials, not blogs
- Decision-makers respond to LinkedIn DMs, not cold emails

Step 2: Design a Small, Fast Test

What's the smallest version of the idea you can test?

- A dummy pricing page with Stripe checkout
- A blog post + video comparison with click tracking
- A LinkedIn message campaign to 50 prospects

Design it with **learning**, not perfection, in mind.

Step 3: Launch to a Real Audience

Testing in isolation is a mistake. You need **external response.** Even 50–100 people is enough for signal.

Don't let perfect targeting be a bottleneck. Imperfect data now beats perfect data never.

Step 4: Define Success Metrics

Before you run it, write this down:

> "If [X people] do [Y action], we'll consider this validated."

Examples:

- If 10 out of 100 visitors click 'Buy Now'
- If 5 prospects book a demo call
- If 20% of users complete onboarding in 24 hours

Step 5: Analyze, Learn, Repeat

When you get the results, look deeper than yes/no. Ask:

- Where did users drop off?
- What feedback came up?
- What didn't happen that we expected?

Then use that insight to plan the next iteration.

Mindset Shift: Embracing Iterative Thinking

To build an iterative culture in yourself or your team, you must challenge three dangerous mindsets:

1. "We have to get this right before we launch."

No. You have to **learn fast** after you launch.

2. "We already know what the customer wants."

You don't. Even if you think you do, test it anyway. You'll be surprised.

3. "We're too small to test like that."

Testing isn't a luxury—it's your survival mechanism. Iteration doesn't require size. It requires discipline.

Real-World Example: Airbnb's Dozen Tiny Iterations

Airbnb didn't start with sleek UX or an explosive launch. In fact, the early version was ugly and buggy.

But they ran micro-experiments constantly:

- Changing photo formats
- Tweaking listing descriptions
- Testing booking flows
- Visiting hosts in person for feedback

Each change was small. But over time, those tiny loops created a product that people trusted.

Without that iteration discipline, Airbnb would have stayed a niche rental site for design conferences.

Your Iteration Blueprint

Here's a template you can use every week:

1. Hypothesis:

We believe that ___ will lead to ___ for ___ users.

2. Experiment:

We will test this by ___ (landing page, email, ad, etc.).

3. Metric for success:

If ___ people do ___, we'll consider it validated.

4. Timeline:

Start: [date]

End: [date]

5. Next steps based on outcomes:

- If successful, we'll ___.
- If inconclusive, we'll ___.
- If failed, we'll ___.

Make this process routine—not reactive. Do it weekly, not yearly.

The Iterative Edge: Compounding Learning

Here's the best part: iteration compounds.

The more you do it, the better you get. Not just at your product—but at thinking, testing, and responding.

Each loop gives you:

- Better instincts
- Sharper questions
- Faster recovery
- Higher clarity

And over time, your startup becomes an adaptive machine—a living organism that learns faster than the competition.

That's how you win.

Action Steps: Run Your First Iteration Loop

1. Write down one assumption you've made this month.
2. Design an MVE (Minimum Viable Experiment) to test it.
3. Define success before running it.
4. Launch it within 7 days.
5. Review the results and plan the next version.

Closing Thought: Iteration Is Your Superpower

You don't need to be a genius to succeed as an entrepreneur.

You need to be scientific.

- Build to test.
- Measure to learn.
- Learn to grow.

And repeat.

That loop—run with speed, honesty, and consistency—is the real secret to building something great.

You won't just survive the startup journey.

You'll evolve through it.

Chapter 5: The Iteration Cycle — Build, Measure, Learn, Repeat

- How do you structure cycles of building and testing in your projects?
- What tools help you measure progress effectively?
- Can you give an example of a pivot driven by iterative learning?
- How do you maintain momentum across multiple iteration cycles?

CHAPTER 6

Feedback Loops – How to Build a Business That Learns

> *"A system that doesn't learn is a system that dies."* — *Anonymous systems engineer*

Imagine your business as a living, breathing organism. Each moment, it processes inputs—every click on your landing page, every word in a customer review, every bug your engineer logs, every competitor's update. These aren't just "data points." They're opportunities. Each signal contains the seeds of transformation—if you're set up to listen.

Unfortunately, most startups aren't. They operate like deaf machines—repeating processes blindly, optimizing the wrong things, or ignoring what their customers are actually trying to say. They build faster, not smarter. And in the end, they burn out.

Scientific entrepreneurs think differently. They don't just act—they observe, interpret, and adapt. They don't just collect feedback—they engineer **feedback loops** into every layer of their business.

Let's break down what that means—and why it's the hidden engine of every resilient, adaptive, and eventually unstoppable company.

🧠 What Is a Feedback Loop?

A feedback loop is a simple concept from systems theory. It's a cyclical process where the outcome of an action feeds back into the system, changing how it behaves next time.

Think of it as nature's update button.

When a thermostat senses that the room is too cold, it triggers the heater. When a cyclist leans too far, their body instinctively adjusts to maintain balance. When animals overgraze a field, vegetation drops, and the herd either migrates or dies off—stabilizing the system again.

In biological systems, mechanical systems, and digital systems, **feedback** is how equilibrium is maintained—or how growth is amplified.

In business, feedback loops serve the same function. They regulate your operations, correct your mistakes, and accelerate what's working.

There are two main types:

- **Negative feedback loops** correct deviations. They stabilize your system. Example: user complaints help you fix onboarding bugs.
- **Positive feedback loops** amplify behaviors. They accelerate momentum. Example: happy users invite others, who invite more, triggering exponential growth.

A healthy business needs both. One for stability. One for scale.

But here's the key: the magic isn't in *getting* feedback. It's in **designing systems** that automatically absorb, interpret, and act on it. That's what makes a business learn.

🔁 Why Feedback Loops Are Essential in Entrepreneurship

Without feedback, you're flying blind.

With bad feedback, you're steering off a cliff

With structured, fast, and meaningful feedback—you're unstoppable.

Startups operate under extreme uncertainty. Every decision—from what to build to how to price—is a hypothesis. Feedback is how you test those hypotheses in the real world.

When you build deliberate feedback loops into your product, team, and market interactions, you create a learning machine. Instead of guessing, you discover. Instead of pushing harder, you push smarter.

Consider these three forces feedback loops unlock:

1. Speed

Fast feedback loops compress your learning cycle. Instead of waiting months to see if a product is working, you get early signals—allowing you to pivot, tweak, or double down before wasting resources.

2. Clarity

Structured feedback cuts through noise. You stop reacting to anecdotes or gut feelings and start acting on patterns and data.

3. Compounding Insight

Every loop generates insight. Every insight makes the next loop smarter. Over time, your business becomes an evolving, adapting intelligence system—like an organism getting stronger with every challenge.

This is not just theoretical. Let's dive deeper into how feedback loops actually work in practice.

🔄 The Anatomy of a Feedback Loop

Every feedback loop follows a simple cycle:

[Action Taken] → [Signal Generated] → [Insight Extracted] → [Adjustment Made] → [Repeat]

Here's a real-world example from a SaaS product:

- A user signs up for your app (Action)
- They bounce during onboarding (Signal)
- You identify friction in the first task (Insight)
- You redesign the onboarding flow (Adjustment)
- New users now get further in the process (New Cycle)

This cycle turns every user interaction into data. Every data point becomes a learning opportunity. And every learning opportunity feeds into action.

Let's break down the four core components of this loop:

1. Trigger

What event kicks off the loop? This could be a user behavior (like abandoning a cart), a team decision (like launching a new feature), or an external shift (like a market change).

2. Signal

What feedback comes from that trigger? Signals can be quantitative (e.g., bounce rate increases) or qualitative (e.g., user complaints).

3. Interpretation

This is where human intelligence—or AI—comes in. What do the signals mean? Are they confirming your hypothesis or challenging it?

4. Response

What do you do with that information? The best loops don't stop at insight. They close the loop by making a change—and measuring the impact.

Simple to describe. Hard to execute well. Why? Because most teams either miss the signals, misinterpret them, or ignore them entirely.

📊 The 5 Critical Feedback Loops Every Startup Needs

Let's get tactical. If you want to build a business that learns, you need to intentionally install feedback loops in key areas.

Here are the five most powerful:

1. Customer Behavior Loop

This loop tracks how users interact with your product.

- **Tool Examples**: Mixpanel, Amplitude, Google Analytics
- **Signal Types**: Clicks, heatmaps, time spent, drop-off points
- **Goal**: Identify friction, optimize flows, improve retention

🧪 *Case Insight*: If 70% of users drop off after the second screen in your app, you don't need a guess—you need to test that screen.

2. Customer Voice Loop

This loop listens to what customers *say*, not just what they *do*.

- **Tool Examples**: Typeform, Intercom, Hotjar surveys
- **Signal Types**: Reviews, NPS scores, interviews
- **Goal**: Understand emotional drivers, unmet needs, hidden frustrations

🧪 *Case Insight*: Airbnb famously used user interviews to uncover emotional gaps in the travel experience, leading to their iconic host review system.

3. Internal Team Loop

Your own people are a goldmine of feedback—if you set up systems for it.

- **Tool Examples**: Notion, Slack retrospectives, Google Forms
- **Signal Types**: Weekly reflections, sprint reviews, culture surveys

- **Goal**: Identify internal friction, improve operations, catch blind spots

🧪 *Case Insight*: Atlassian built a ritual called "Team Health Checks" that lets teams self-assess collaboration and surface issues before they explode.

4. Product Quality Loop

This loop captures bugs, errors, and technical issues—turning failures into fixes.

- **Tool Examples**: Jira, Sentry, GitHub Issues
- **Signal Types**: Bug reports, error logs, crash data
- **Goal**: Improve stability, reduce churn, increase confidence

🧪 *Case Insight*: Stripe's obsession with bug feedback loops led to legendary reliability. Their engineers track and fix issues *before* users report them.

5. Market Trend Loop

The world changes. Your competitors evolve. This loop ensures you don't fall behind.

- **Tool Examples**: Reddit, X (formerly Twitter), G2, Substack newsletters
- **Signal Types**: Competitor features, user complaints, trend analysis
- **Goal**: Spot opportunities, avoid irrelevance, inspire innovation

🧪 *Case Insight*: Canva constantly monitors design trends and integrates new templates and styles based on evolving user needs.

📈 Case Study: Superhuman's Relentless Feedback System

Superhuman, the ultra-fast email app, didn't launch until they hit **Product-Market Fit**—measured *scientifically*.

They asked every user:

> "How would you feel if you could no longer use Superhuman?"

They categorized responses:

- Very disappointed
- Somewhat disappointed
- Not disappointed

Only when **40% said "very disappointed"** did they scale. Why?

Because that's the threshold where loyalty becomes growth. But they didn't stop there. They:

- Interviewed the "very disappointed" group
- Prioritized features only they wanted
- Built for their most passionate users

This wasn't guesswork. It was a feedback loop engineered into their core.

Result? Sky-high retention. Product evangelists. Premium brand positioning.

🛠 How to Build Feedback Loops Into Your Company (Step-by-Step)

Let's bring this home. Here's a repeatable framework to install learning loops into your startup:

Step 1: Choose a Focus Area

Start small. Pick one critical function:

- Onboarding
- Pricing
- Landing page
- Customer service

- Team processes

Step 2: Instrument It

Add sensors to capture behavior. This could mean:

- Event tracking (e.g., sign-up funnel)
- Surveys (e.g., post-support satisfaction)
- Interviews (e.g., user testing)

Step 3: Schedule Reflection

Make feedback interpretation a weekly habit:

- What confused users this week?
- What underperformed?
- What hypothesis failed?

Step 4: Close the Loop

Act on the insight. Run a test. Ship a change. And measure the result.

Step 5: Systematize

Automate data collection. Build dashboards. Create rituals. Don't rely on memory—rely on systems.

❌ What Destroys Feedback Loops?

Even great teams mess this up. Here's what to watch out for:

- **Ego** – Refusing to accept uncomfortable truths
- **Inaction** – Collecting data but not doing anything with it
- **Overload** – Drowning in metrics without prioritizing
- **Vanity** – Obsessing over likes instead of outcomes

Good feedback loops are:

- Fast
- Focused
- Actionable

The tighter your loop, the faster your evolution.

🧠 Exercise: Map One Feedback Loop Now

Take 10 minutes and apply this:

- What's one key user behavior you care about?
- What signals indicate success or failure?
- What tool captures that?
- When do you review it?
- What's your next experiment?

You don't need a PhD to do this. You just need a pen and discipline.

🚀 Closing Thought: The Startup That Learns Wins

Startups fail not because they move too slowly—but because they learn too slowly.

You don't need more funding, more features, or more hype.

You need tighter feedback loops.

The faster you learn, the faster you adapt.

The faster you adapt, the harder you are to kill.

Scientific entrepreneurs aren't just builders.

They're systems designers.

They architect businesses that evolve faster than the market.

Because in the end, entrepreneurship isn't just an execution game.

It's a learning game.

And feedback loops are how you win it.

Chapter 6: Feedback Loops — How to Build a Business That Learns

- What feedback channels have been most effective for your team?
- How do you ensure feedback is acted on promptly?
- Can you share how feedback loops improved a product or service?
- How do you balance internal vs. external feedback for decision-making?

CHAPTER 7

Actionable Metrics — Measuring What Matters

> *"Without data, you're just another person with an opinion." — W. Edwards Deming*

In the world of entrepreneurship, what gets measured truly does get managed—but only if you're measuring the right things. Metrics guide decision-making, shape strategy, and illuminate progress. Yet many entrepreneurs fall into the trap of collecting data without insight. They obsess over numbers that look impressive but provide little direction—what we call *vanity metrics*. In contrast, *actionable metrics* offer clarity, causality, and a path forward. This chapter dives into the critical difference between these two types of metrics, shows how to design measurement systems that matter, and illustrates how companies like Airbnb and Dropbox used metrics to accelerate learning and growth.

The Dangerous Allure of Vanity Metrics

Vanity metrics are numbers that look good on a pitch deck but don't help you make better decisions. These include total downloads, registered users, page views, or media mentions—figures that might impress investors but often lack correlation with real business health. While these metrics can offer psychological comfort and fuel PR stories, they rarely tell you what's working or what to fix.

Imagine a startup with 100,000 app downloads. At first glance, that sounds like success. But what if only 1,000 of those users open the app more than once? And what if just 100 ever make a purchase? Suddenly, the headline number collapses under scrutiny. Worse, it can mislead founders into thinking they're on the right path.

Vanity metrics create a false sense of achievement. They're appealing because they're easy to grow through marketing spend or manipulation, but they don't validate the business model or guide product iteration.

The Power of Actionable Metrics

Actionable metrics are the opposite of vanity metrics. They help you make informed decisions because they are tied to user behavior, outcomes, and hypotheses. These metrics show cause and effect, allowing you to draw a line between your actions and their consequences.

For a metric to be actionable, it must be:

1. **Tied to a specific behavior** (e.g., purchases, engagement, referrals).
2. **Cohort-based** rather than cumulative, allowing clear comparison across time.
3. **Controllable through experimentation**, so you can change an input and observe the output.

For example, instead of tracking total sign-ups, a SaaS company might track the percentage of users who activate within 24 hours, return on day 7, and convert to paid by day 30. These metrics are narrow but deeply insightful, revealing the effectiveness of onboarding, retention, and monetization strategies.

Case Study: Dropbox's Viral Loop and Metrics

Dropbox, the cloud storage pioneer, famously grew through a viral referral program. But this wasn't a lucky accident—it was engineered, measured, and iterated scientifically.

They didn't just count new users. Instead, they asked: How many users referred a friend? What percentage of those referrals led to sign-ups? How many of those sign-ups uploaded a file (activation)?

Dropbox's team closely monitored the following actionable metrics:

- Referral invite conversion rate
- Activation rate post-sign-up
- Storage usage over time
- Churn rate across cohorts

When they tested changes to referral incentives (e.g., more free storage for inviting friends), they could immediately measure the impact across these KPIs. This allowed them to fine-tune the system, improve the viral coefficient, and achieve explosive growth without massive ad spend.

Key takeaway: They measured behavior, not just user counts, enabling precise optimization.

Case Study: Airbnb's Marketplace Efficiency

Airbnb, in its early stages, didn't just look at booking growth. The founders cared deeply about the *matching efficiency* of their marketplace—how well supply (hosts) and demand (guests) connected.

Instead of tracking aggregate listings, they measured:

- Listing conversion rate (views to bookings)
- Time to first booking
- Response rate and time by hosts
- Booking window preferences by region

This attention to matching quality led to experiments like professional photography for listings, which they found increased booking rates significantly. These insights came from analyzing detailed cohort and funnel data, not from surface-level user metrics.

By focusing on marketplace health indicators, Airbnb improved trust, increased transaction volume, and ensured sustainable growth.

Leading vs Lagging Indicators

Understanding the difference between *leading* and *lagging* indicators is critical when designing your measurement strategy.

- **Lagging indicators** show what *has already happened* (e.g., revenue, churn).
- **Leading indicators** are predictive signals that precede those outcomes (e.g., daily active usage, engagement scores).

To manage a startup effectively, you need both—but leading indicators are more powerful in shaping decisions.

For instance, if your churn rate spikes, it's too late to fix what caused it. But if you notice a decline in weekly engagement, that's a red flag you can act on immediately.

A good framework is to tie every lagging indicator (like revenue) to one or more leading indicators (like conversion rate or active users per cohort), and to use those to test and steer your experiments.

Designing Actionable Metrics

Here's a step-by-step guide to developing actionable metrics in your startup:

1. **Start with a hypothesis:** What belief are you testing? E.g., "Users who complete onboarding are more likely to retain."
2. **Define a measurable behavior:** Choose behaviors that can confirm or falsify the hypothesis: e.g., "percentage of users who return on Day 7 after completing onboarding."

3. **Use cohorts, not cumulative stats:** Analyze users based on when they joined or took an action to understand patterns over time.
4. **Track behavior change after interventions:** Run A/B tests or rollouts to see how a change affects the target metric.
5. **Avoid ratios without context:** Metrics like "bounce rate" or "monthly active users" are only meaningful when tied to behavior or compared across cohorts.
6. **Automate data hygiene:** Ensure consistent, clean, and timely data so you're not making decisions based on noise.

The Metrics Pyramid

To prioritize what you measure, it helps to visualize your metrics in a pyramid structure:

1. **North Star Metric (NSM):** The one metric that captures the core value delivered (e.g., for Slack: messages sent per team).
2. **Key Drivers:** Inputs that influence the NSM (e.g., onboarding success rate, number of active users).
3. **Diagnostic Metrics:** Deeper-level analytics that explain changes in drivers (e.g., time to first response, channel invites sent).

This hierarchy keeps your team aligned on impact while enabling precision when things go wrong.

Cautionary Tale: WeWork's Metric Mirage

WeWork, once a $47 billion startup, offers a cautionary tale in misusing metrics. The company touted massive revenue growth and global expansion as signs of dominance. But beneath the surface, it ignored critical actionable metrics like:

- Profit per location
- Utilization rate

- Lifetime value vs customer acquisition cost (LTV:CAC)

Instead, it leaned into vanity: number of cities, headcount, capital raised. This lack of actionable focus led to unsustainable operations, high burn, and eventually a near-collapse.

Lesson: Even fast-growing companies must ground themselves in meaningful metrics tied to unit economics and real user behavior.

Building a Metrics-Driven Culture

Creating a culture that respects and uses actionable data requires:

- **Leadership buy-in:** Founders must model data-informed decision-making.
- **Transparency:** Share metrics openly with the team.
- **Tools and dashboards:** Invest early in tools like Mixpanel, Amplitude, or Looker to ensure access to quality data.
- **Education:** Teach your team how to interpret data and what good metrics look like.
- **Accountability:** Tie experiments and OKRs to metric outcomes, not just tasks.

Scientific Entrepreneurship Means Measurable Experiments

At the heart of the scientific approach is the feedback loop: hypothesize, test, measure, learn, repeat. Actionable metrics are the backbone of this loop. They allow entrepreneurs to identify which experiments worked, which failed, and where to go next.

In practice:

- Before launching a new feature, define the success metric.
- During rollout, track the leading indicators of adoption and usage.
- Afterward, analyze retention, NPS, and behavior change across cohorts.

This method transforms guesswork into a learning system—and learning is the real engine of innovation.

Final Thoughts: What You Measure Is What You Become

Metrics shape culture. They influence what teams prioritize, celebrate, and improve. By choosing actionable over vanity metrics, you turn your startup into a learning machine—where every initiative is an experiment, every experiment teaches something, and every lesson drives growth.

You don't need more data. You need better data. Data that speaks to behavior, drives decisions, and tells the story of what's working—and what's not.

Measure what matters, ignore what dazzles, and let your metrics be your compass, not your comfort.

📊 Chapter 7 — Measuring What Matters

Choose one:

- Replace one vanity metric you're tracking with an actionable metric. Write down what decision it will help you make.
- Create a mini dashboard (even on paper) that tracks only metrics tied to user behavior or business learning.

Chapter 7: Actionable Metrics — Measuring What Matters

- How do you identify which metrics truly reflect progress?
- What's your approach to avoiding vanity metrics?
- Can you share an example where data influenced a major decision?
- How do you communicate key metrics to stakeholders?

CHAPTER 8

Experiment Like a Scientist — Turning Uncertainty into Progress

"In theory, there's no difference between theory and practice. In practice, there is." — *Yogi Berra*

Entrepreneurship is not a linear journey. It is not a map with well-marked trails or a destination with predictable weather. It's a foggy expedition filled with guesswork, false turns, limited visibility, and unexpected discoveries. In this environment, certainty is a luxury—and clarity must be earned.

So how do you move forward when you're unsure of what lies ahead?

You experiment.

And not haphazardly. Not randomly. Not by throwing spaghetti against the wall.

You experiment like a scientist.

Science, like entrepreneurship, is a discipline built on uncertainty. The difference is how that uncertainty is handled. While most people fear it or ignore it, scientists turn it into a tool—a gateway to discovery. By applying the same structured thinking, founders can transform chaotic guesses into controlled learning.

This chapter explores how to design and run business experiments using the scientific method—not as a metaphor, but as a process to iterate, validate, and grow your venture.

🔬 The Scientific Method, Simplified

Let's start at the source.

The scientific method has guided centuries of discovery and innovation. It's elegant, clear, and shockingly underused in business. Here's the classic structure:

1. **Observation** – What do you notice?
2. **Hypothesis** – What do you think is true?
3. **Experiment** – How will you test that belief?
4. **Data Collection** – What happens when you test?
5. **Analysis** – What did the results reveal?
6. **Conclusion** – Was your hypothesis supported?
7. **Iteration** – What will you test next?

In a lab, this process led to penicillin, relativity, and DNA sequencing.

In a startup, it leads to product-market fit, breakthrough features, and scalable marketing.

The tools are different—but the thinking is the same. And that thinking is what matters most.

🧪 From Lab to Launch: Translating Science into Startups

How do we take this method and apply it to real startup life?

Here's how each scientific step maps to a startup context:

Scientific Step	Startup Equivalent
Observation	Market research, user behavior, customer feedback
Hypothesis	A specific belief about your product or customer
Experiment	A landing page, feature rollout, marketing test
Data Collection	Analytics, interviews, A/B test results
Analysis	What worked? What didn't? Why?
Conclusion	Kill, keep, or double down
Iteration	Plan the next test

This is not a one-time activity. It is a cycle—a loop you run weekly, even daily.

Great companies don't grow by perfect launches. They grow by compounding insight.

🎯 Start with a Good Hypothesis

The foundation of every good experiment is a strong hypothesis. And unfortunately, most startup hypotheses are terrible.

Bad Hypothesis:

"People will love our app."

(Vague, emotional, untestable.)

Good Hypothesis:

"If we offer a 14-day free trial, 30% of visitors will sign up within a week."

(Specific, measurable, actionable.)

To craft better hypotheses, ask yourself:

- What do I believe users want?
- How would I see that belief reflected in their actions?

- What behavior would validate or disprove it?

Then refine until your hypothesis is something a scientist would approve of. A good one is falsifiable—it can be proven wrong. This is a feature, not a bug.

👉 Designing Your First Real Business Experiment

Here's a lightweight, reusable framework for business experiments:

Goal: What are we trying to learn?

→ e.g., "Understand if pricing is a major barrier to signups."

Hypothesis:

→ "Lowering the price by 20% will increase conversions by 15%."

Test Method:

→ Run an A/B test between the original price and the discounted price.

Measurement Plan:

→ Track conversion rate over 7 days, targeting 1,000 unique visits.

Success Criteria:

→ If the lower price converts ≥15% better with statistical confidence, we win.

Simple. Focused. Actionable.

The key is isolation—test one variable at a time. Otherwise, you won't know what caused the change.

⚠️ Common Experiment Mistakes (and How to Avoid Them)

Even with a great framework, most founders fall into predictable traps. Here are the big ones:

- **Testing too many things at once:** You learn nothing. Keep it surgical.
- **Not enough data:** A few dozen users won't give you signal. Aim for statistical significance.
- **Running inconclusive tests:** Design with clear criteria. Know what will count as a win.
- **Ignoring the results:** If you're not going to act on the outcome, don't waste time testing it.
- **Biasing the data:** Let go of ego. Look for truth, not validation.

Remember: the goal isn't to be right. It's to learn something useful—fast.

🔁 Experiments as Growth Loops

A single experiment isn't the goal. A system of experiments is.

Each test you run should trigger a decision:

✅ Validated → Build more of it

❌ Invalidated → Kill or rethink it

🫤 Inconclusive → Refine and retest

When you do this continuously, you create a growth loop—a repeatable engine for insight and acceleration.

Startups that scale don't have all the answers. They just run more experiments and get to answers faster.

Case Study: Dropbox and the MVP Video

Dropbox, now a multi-billion-dollar file sharing company, didn't begin by building a complex system.

Instead, they made a 2-minute explainer video showing what the product *would* do.

The result?

- Tens of thousands of signups.
- A massive waitlist.
- Validation that people *wanted* this solution.

All before writing the backend infrastructure.

Lesson: The best experiments are fast, cheap, and reveal demand early.

Case Study: Airbnb's Photo Experiment

In 2009, **Airbnb** noticed a problem—many listings weren't getting booked. After inspecting the data, they saw a trend: low-quality photos correlated with fewer bookings.

So they ran a simple test.

They hired professional photographers to retake images of a small batch of listings in New York.

Result?

Bookings *doubled* in those listings. The experiment proved the value of quality visuals.

Today, Airbnb still offers free photography in some cities.

Lesson: A single data-driven test can shift a product roadmap.

🧠 Mental Model: The Experimentation Flywheel

Think of your business like a lab. Each test you run spins the flywheel faster:

1. **Ask** – What's the biggest unknown right now?
2. **Test** – Run a simple, focused experiment.
3. **Learn** – Analyze the outcome, however it lands.
4. **Act** – Adjust your product, strategy, or messaging.
5. **Repeat** – Every week.
6. This builds momentum. Each spin leads to sharper hypotheses, better insights, and more growth.

💼 Mini Exercise: Design Your First Experiment

Take a moment. Think of one thing you're unsure about in your business. Then fill this out:

🎯 What do I want to learn?

→ ______________________________________

💡 What's my hypothesis?

→ ______________________________________

🧪 What will I test?

→ ______________________________________

📈 What will I measure?

→ ______________________________________

✅ What's my success criteria?

→ ______________________________________

Set a date. Run it this week. Then review. You'll be amazed how much clarity one small test can create.

🧠 Case Study: Buffer's Pricing Test

Buffer, the social media scheduling app, wasn't sure how much to charge. Rather than guess, they ran a live pricing test on their website.

They showed three pricing options to different visitors and tracked conversion.

From this data, they chose a price point that maximized revenue *and* signup rate.

No focus group. No speculation. Just data.

Lesson: If you're unsure, test. Don't guess.

🌱 Closing Thought: Learn Loudly, Fail Quietly

The entrepreneurs who win aren't the ones who guess correctly.

They're the ones who **learn faster** than everyone else.

Your business is a hypothesis. Your roadmap is a lab notebook. Your job is to uncover truth—not just build stuff.

Every landing page, feature, ad, email, or price point is an experiment waiting to happen.

Don't wait for certainty. Don't hope for brilliance.

Test. Learn. Adjust. Repeat.

That's how scientists made progress for centuries. That's how you'll make progress too.

Be humble in your assumptions.

Be disciplined in your method.

Be relentless in your learning.

Chapter 8: Experiment Like a Scientist — Turning Uncertainty into Progress

- **How do you plan experiments under conditions of uncertainty?**
- **What practices keep your tests rigorous and unbiased?**
- **Can you describe how you interpret conflicting experiment results?**
- **How do you decide when an experiment is worth scaling?**

CHAPTER 9

Think in Loops, Not Lines – Mastering Iterative Mindsets

> *"It's not about being right. It's about becoming less wrong, faster." — Paul Saffo*

🔍 The Illusion of Straight Lines

From an early age, we're taught that success is a straight line:

1. Make a plan
2. Execute the plan
3. Achieve the goal

In school, you study the syllabus, pass the test, and move on. In many jobs, you're handed a process and expected to follow it. The idea is comforting — if you follow the steps, you'll reach the destination.

But entrepreneurship doesn't work that way.

In the world of startups, the terrain shifts beneath your feet. Customers behave unpredictably, competitors pivot suddenly, and the market rewrites its rules in real-time. No matter how brilliant your initial plan, it's only a guess until it's tested by reality.

Linear thinking, while useful for stable systems, fails in environments of high uncertainty. Startups are not machines — they're learning organisms. In this chaos, the best entrepreneurs don't seek perfect plans. They seek **fast feedback**.

To thrive, you must replace straight lines with **loops**.

🔄 Loop Thinking: The Core of Scientific Entrepreneurship

The entrepreneurial process is iterative by nature. Rather than betting everything on a grand launch, successful founders **test, learn, and adapt continuously**. They run tight feedback cycles and let reality reshape their ideas.

At the heart of this loop-based mindset is a simple sequence:

1. **Build** – Create a minimum viable version of your idea.
2. **Measure** – Observe real-world feedback and collect data.
3. **Learn** – Analyze results to understand what worked and what didn't.
4. **Iterate** – Adjust, improve, and run the cycle again.

This isn't a one-time event. It's a **repeating system of refinement**. Each pass through the loop moves you closer to something that works.

The secret is not to avoid being wrong. It's to **get less wrong, faster**.

Linear vs. Iterative Thinking: A Side-by-Side Comparison

Mindset	Linear Thinking	Loop Thinking
Planning	Rigid, up-front strategy	Adaptive, evolving insights
Assumptions	Must be right from the start	Tested and refined over time
Risk	High – all-in bets	Lower – small, testable steps
Failure	Final, to be avoided	Informative, part of learning
Speed	Slow to start, slower to adapt	Fast feedback, fast correction

Loop thinking transforms how you approach every part of your business. You stop trying to get it perfect up front, and instead design your system to improve relentlessly over time.

📷 Case Study: Instagram — From Clutter to Clarity

Instagram started as **Burbn**, a location-based check-in app overloaded with features: photos, plans, friends, rewards, messages. It tried to do everything — and users didn't know what to do with it.

But the founders noticed something curious: people consistently used just one feature — sharing photos.

So they **looped**.

- **Observation:** Photo-sharing gets traction.
- **Build:** Strip the app to only one function: photo sharing.
- **Measure:** User engagement and growth spike.
- **Learn:** Simplicity outperforms complexity.
- **Iterate:** Add filters, improve sharing, refine UX.

Within weeks, Burbn was rebranded and relaunched as **Instagram**. One focused feature became a viral success.

This wasn't luck. It was disciplined iteration.

📺 Case Study: Netflix — Reinvention on Repeat

Netflix could have remained a DVD mailing company. That model was working. But they didn't cling to the original idea.

Instead, they looped:

1. **Tested streaming** before it was mainstream.
2. **Analyzed viewing habits** to refine recommendations.
3. **Produced original content** based on insights.
4. **Experimented** with show formats and release strategies.

Each decision was a result of controlled loops:

- Hypothesis: Will users binge entire seasons?
- Test: Release House of Cards all at once.

- Result: Massive engagement.
- Iteration: Expand the model with Stranger Things, Narcos, and more.

Netflix didn't just react to trends — they **created them**, by iterating faster than their competitors.

🔄 Loop Thinking for Every Function

Loop-based thinking is not just for product teams. It applies across the entire business:

🎯 Product Development

- MVP → Feedback → Refine → Relaunch
- Avoid feature bloat; build only what solves a validated problem.

📢 Marketing

- Message → Campaign → Results → Refine Message
- Test hooks, copy, and formats before scaling.

💼 Sales

- Pitch → Objection → Revise Pitch → Re-test
- Turn rejections into insight, not discouragement.

🧭 Strategy

- Vision → Small bets → Market reaction → Adjust direction
- Strategy isn't a plan—it's a **series of intelligent loops**.

Every department is a lab. Every decision is a test.

📈 Compounding Loops = Exponential Learning

Think of each loop as a **unit of learning**.

The more loops you complete:

- The more assumptions you test,
- The more risks you eliminate,
- The more clarity you gain.

And here's the magic: **loops compound.**

- **Loop 1:** You kill a flawed idea early.
- **Loop 5:** You find a sticky feature.
- **Loop 12:** You unlock a scalable growth channel.
- **Loop 30:** You dominate a market niche.

Just like compound interest builds wealth, **compound learning builds momentum**. Your product, team, and insight all evolve faster than competitors stuck in rigid plans.

⚠ What Kills Iteration?

Even founders who embrace experimentation often fall into traps:

✖ Big Launch Syndrome

- Waiting too long to release anything.
- Fear of shipping something imperfect.

✖ Hypothesis Drift

- Testing too many variables at once.
- Vague goals lead to vague outcomes.

✖ Data Blindness

- Cherry-picking results that confirm biases.
- Ignoring inconvenient truths.

✖ Ego Attachment

- Falling in love with your idea.
- Resisting feedback that contradicts your vision.

These mistakes don't just slow you down — they **distort your loops** and waste your most valuable resource: **time to learn**.

🛠️ Mini Exercise – Audit Your Thinking Style

Choose a current project. Answer the following:

- ❓ Have I tested the core assumption yet?
- 📊 What's one piece of real data I could gather this week?
- 🔁 How quickly can I run a small loop to learn something new?

Now fill this out:

🎯 **Hypothesis:** ______________________________

🧪 **Test:** ______________________________

📈 **Metric:** ______________________________

✅ **Success Criteria:** ______________________________

Run the test. Let the data speak.

🏗️ Loop-Driven Culture: Build the Right Environment

If you want to build a company that thrives on iteration, you need to **design the culture to support it**:

- **Celebrate learning**, not just wins.
- **Reward fast experiments**, even if they fail.
- **Hire adaptable thinkers**, not just plan executors.
- **Document learnings**, so loops don't repeat unnecessarily.

Build a team that doesn't just do loops — but **thinks** in loops.

💡 Real-World Loop Thinkers

Here are some standout examples of leaders and teams who mastered iterative mindsets:

✅ Airbnb

Early users were not booking. The team hand-photographed apartments to improve listings. Bookings shot up. Lesson: iterate on the value **customers perceive**, not just what you provide.

✅ Duolingo

The app constantly A/B tests everything from button colors to onboarding steps. It's a loop machine disguised as a language app.

✅ Superhuman

They onboard each user manually to understand pain points. Their loop is human-powered — but incredibly focused on learning.

🧠 Closing Thought: Loops Are Your Superpower

In an unpredictable world, straight lines are an illusion. Business success is not a destination — it's an **ongoing process of becoming less wrong, faster**.

The best entrepreneurs:

- Don't wait for perfect conditions.
- Don't rely on grand plans.
- Don't guess what users want.

They **loop**.

They act, learn, and adjust — again and again, until reality tells them what works.

'When in doubt, loop it out.'

Chapter 9: Think in Loops, Not Lines — Mastering Iterative Mindsets

- How do you shift from linear to nonlinear thinking in projects?
- Can you give an example of a system you built that adapts over time?
- How do loops help in managing complexity in your work?
- What challenges arise when adopting iterative mindsets?

CHAPTER 10

The Hypothesis Mindset – Thinking Like a Scientist

> *"In questions of science, the authority of a thousand is not worth the humble reasoning of a single individual."*
> *— Galileo Galilei*

🧠 The Invisible Danger: Assumptions Disguised as Facts

Entrepreneurs are natural optimists. They move fast, trust their instincts, and chase big visions. That spirit is powerful — but it can also be perilous. Behind every startup pitch, product launch, or marketing campaign lurks a quiet threat: **unquestioned assumptions**.

We assume:

- "Our product is more intuitive."
- "People will pay for this because they're already doing X."
- "This feature will go viral."
- "Our customers behave rationally."

Assumptions are not inherently bad. In fact, you can't build anything new without making a few leaps. But the real danger lies in mistaking assumptions for **facts** — in believing without testing.

Here's the hard truth:

> Most entrepreneurs fail not because they lacked vision — but because they built on untested assumptions.

Scientific entrepreneurs see this differently. They recognize that every idea, every belief, every prediction is just a **hypothesis** — a statement that must earn its truth through testing.

What Is a Hypothesis?

In science, a hypothesis is not a wild guess. It's a precise, testable statement about cause and effect, based on logic or observation.

A good hypothesis in business follows this format:

> "If we [do this], then [this result] will happen because [reason]."

Example:

"If we shorten our sign-up form from five fields to two, then completion rates will increase by 20% because we've reduced user friction."

This statement has three critical components:

1. **Action:** The intervention (e.g., shortening the form).
2. **Outcome:** The predicted result (e.g., higher completion rate).
3. **Reason:** The rationale behind the expected effect (e.g., lower friction).

Why does this matter?

Because **a hypothesis is falsifiable** — you can run a test and find out whether it holds up. If it doesn't, you've learned something vital. If it does, you've earned evidence to move forward with confidence.

⚠ Bad Hypotheses vs. Good Ones

The quality of your thinking shows up in the quality of your hypotheses. Let's compare:

✗ Weak Hypothesis	✅ Strong Hypothesis
"Customers will love our new design."	"If we implement design X, our Net Promoter Score (NPS) will improve by 15% in 3 weeks because users find it simpler."
"This ad will go viral."	"If we include a provocative question in the first line, the click-through rate will rise by 10% because it triggers curiosity."
"People hate waiting."	"If we reduce load time by 3 seconds, bounce rate will fall by 25% because fewer users will abandon."

Bad hypotheses are vague, emotional, and non-measurable. Good hypotheses are **specific, testable, and tied to a business outcome.**

🧪 Business Is a Lab – Design Your Experiments

If you think like a scientist, then your business becomes a **lab** — and every product decision, marketing campaign, or pricing change is an **experiment**.

Sample Business Hypothesis:

> "If we offer a 7-day free trial instead of a 14-day one, conversions to paid will increase by 15% because users are more likely to make a decision with a tighter deadline."

To test this, you design an A/B experiment:

Component	Description
Test Group	1,000 new users offered a 7-day trial
Control Group	1,000 new users offered a 14-day trial
Metric	% of users who upgrade to paid
Timeframe	30 days
Success Criteria	15% or more increase in conversions in test group

At the end of the test:

- ✅ If results support the hypothesis: consider rolling out the change.
- ❌ If results don't: revise the hypothesis or explore alternative explanations.

The goal is not to be right.

> The goal is to reduce uncertainty and accelerate learning.

The Hypothesis Mindset in Action

The hypothesis mindset doesn't wait until the company is big. It's valuable **from day one** — in fact, it's what enables startups to survive the uncertainty of early-stage chaos.

Step-by-step approach:

1. **Spot the Assumption** – What are we assuming that might not be true?
2. **Form a Hypothesis** – Turn the assumption into a testable statement.
3. **Design an Experiment** – Define your variables, controls, and success metrics.
4. **Run It Quickly** – Use scrappy methods: landing pages, mockups, concierge MVPs.
5. **Capture Results** – What did the data say? Not your gut — the data.
6. **Learn & Adjust** – Do we pivot, persevere, or retest?

This process isn't a one-time thing. It's **continuous** — baked into every part of your business.

Why Entrepreneurs Struggle with This

There's a reason this mindset is rare: it's **emotionally hard**.

- We want to believe our ideas are right.

- We fear being wrong, especially in front of teams or investors.
- We mistake momentum for progress.
- We value intuition over validation.

But science teaches us this:

> Being wrong is not failure. Refusing to test is.

💼 Real-World Case Study: Buffer's Early Pricing Test

Before Buffer built its full platform, the team wanted to know one thing:

Will people pay for this?

Instead of building the product, they built a simple landing page with three pricing plans. When users clicked to subscribe, a message popped up:

> "Thanks! We're not ready yet — but we'll let you know when we are."

They weren't selling anything. They were testing a **hypothesis**:

> "People will click to pay for a social media scheduling tool."

The results were clear:

✅ Enough people clicked on paid plans to validate the demand.

So they moved forward with development — now backed by real evidence, not just intuition.

📺 Case Study: YouTube's Monetization Experiment

In the mid-2000s, YouTube exploded in popularity — but it wasn't clear how to make money from user-generated videos. The early assumption was:

> "People won't tolerate ads on videos."

Instead of assuming, YouTube tested it. They ran experiments with **pre-roll ads** on a small segment of videos and closely watched retention rates.

Surprisingly, users didn't drop off — especially when the ads were skippable after a few seconds. This led to the development of YouTube's **AdSense** system and a multibillion-dollar revenue model.

What started as a fragile hypothesis became the cornerstone of YouTube's business model.

📊 Case Study: Intuit's Culture of Testing

Intuit, makers of TurboTax and QuickBooks, institutionalized the hypothesis mindset.

They embedded **lean experimentation** across product and design teams, even training employees in hypothesis writing. Their internal mantra became:

> "You can't be sure, but you can test your way forward."

One famous test: changing a single word on a call-to-action button increased revenue by millions of dollars. Another involved testing onboarding flows that reduced customer drop-off by 30%.

The company doesn't just build features — it builds **evidence**.

Hypotheses Everywhere – Not Just Product

Think this mindset is just for developers? Think again.

Strategy

"If we focus on SMBs instead of enterprise, our sales cycle will shrink by 40% because decision-making is faster."

Marketing

"If we run webinars instead of blog content, lead conversion will increase by 25% because we're creating live engagement."

Pricing

"If we introduce a 'freemium' tier, overall revenue will increase because of higher funnel volume."

Hiring

"If we use project-based hiring tests, our candidate quality will rise because we'll screen for skill over résumé polish."

The hypothesis mindset is universal. It creates **evidence-driven culture** — one where ego steps back and truth steps forward.

Mini Exercise – Write and Test a Hypothesis

Choose any part of your current business.

Now fill this out:

If we ____,

then ____,

because ____________________________________.

Example:

If we shorten the onboarding process from 10 minutes to 3,

then retention after Day 1 will improve by 15%,

because users experience value faster.

Next:

- 🧪 What's the smallest way to test this?
- 📊 What metric will show if it worked?
- ⏰ What's the time frame for results?

Then run it. Don't just discuss it. Don't overbuild.

Act like a scientist.

🧠 Closing Thought: Belief Is Cheap. Evidence Is Power.

Startups live or die on how fast they learn.

And learning happens not from **being right**, but from being **curious enough to test**.

> "Assumptions feel safe. Hypotheses keep you sharp."

Entrepreneurs who think like scientists:

- Test more ideas, faster.
- Kill bad ideas earlier.
- Double down on proven ones.
- Build cultures of inquiry, not certainty.

They don't need to be right all the time — they need to get less wrong, faster.

So build your hypothesis muscle.

Write them. Run them. Learn from them.

It's not magic. It's just method.

And in the world of startups, method beats myth every time.

Chapter 10: The Hypothesis Mindset — Thinking Like a Scientist

- How do you translate business problems into testable assumptions?
- What frameworks support keeping hypotheses clear and adaptable?
- Can you share how disproving a hypothesis led to innovation?
- How do you maintain curiosity when experiments don't go as planned?

CHAPTER 11

Systems Over Goals – Building Sustainable Success

"You do not rise to the level of your goals. You fall to the level of your systems." — James Clear, Atomic Habits

🎯 The Goal Illusion

Goals are seductive. They're the banners we wave, the dreams we declare, and the finish lines we imagine crossing. Entrepreneurs often set grand visions at the start of their journey:

- "I want to make $1 million in revenue."
- "I want to build the next big app."
- "I want to become the best in my industry."

These goals are powerful. They inspire ambition and ignite action. But they also come with a hidden trap: **they're not how success is actually built**.

A goal is a desired result — an outcome you wish to achieve. But wanting an outcome doesn't get you there. **You don't achieve success by focusing on what you want. You achieve it by focusing on what you do consistently.**

This is the great illusion: that success is the product of goals. In reality, success is the product of systems.

The Truth Behind the Goal

Let's break down the problem.

Imagine two founders who both have the same goal: to launch a profitable startup. One writes it on the whiteboard and visualizes success. The other builds a weekly routine of talking to users, testing hypotheses, shipping features, and measuring feedback. A year later, who is more likely to have a successful product?

Goals may set the direction, but systems set the pace.

That's the fundamental mindset shift of the scientific entrepreneur:

Focus less on what you want, and more on the process that creates it.

🛠 What Is a System?

A system is a **repeatable process**. It's a structured method of doing things that removes guesswork, decision fatigue, and randomness.

In business terms, a system is:

- A workflow
- A habit
- A calendar structure
- A feedback loop
- A routine that drives action

In short, a system is how you show up consistently.

Let's contrast goals and systems with some simple examples:

Goal	System
"I want to grow my YouTube channel."	"I film and publish a new video every Wednesday."
"I want to get more sales."	"I email 20 leads per day and follow up after 3 days."

“I want to stay updated on trends.”	“I read one new case study every Friday morning.”

Systems are practical. They focus on what you can control. They are **engineered, not imagined**.

Why Entrepreneurs Fail Without Systems

Most startups don’t fail because the idea was bad. They fail because the execution was inconsistent.

They start strong, inspired by goals. But when reality gets hard — when the excitement fades — there’s nothing in place to keep them moving. They rely on willpower, and willpower is a limited resource.

Common signs of goal-driven failure:

- Burnout from chasing big milestones
- Constant pivoting without process
- Progress stalls without clear next steps
- Lost momentum when enthusiasm fades

Now let’s contrast that with what systems provide:

- Momentum without motivation
- Clarity on what to do next
- Measurable learning loops
- Resilience through hard weeks

The scientific entrepreneur **designs behaviors that compound**, not ambitions that fluctuate.

Systems Create Compounding Results

The real power of systems is that they **compound**.

Think about compound interest in finance. Small deposits, made regularly, grow exponentially over time. Systems work the same way in business.

Let's do the math:

- Writing 500 words/day = 182,500 words/year (3 books!)
- Sending 5 cold emails/day = 1,825 sales leads/year
- Fixing 1 bug or UX issue/week = 52 quality improvements/year
- Improving onboarding by 1% per week = ~67% better by year's end

These gains aren't flashy. They aren't exciting headlines. But they're unbeatable over time.

Most people overestimate what they can do in a day, but underestimate what they can do in a year — especially with systems in place.

🔬 System Example: The Scientific Experiment Routine

Let's apply this to something we've already covered: hypothesis testing.

You don't just "want to learn what users like." That's a goal. Instead, you create a **testing system** that guarantees you learn consistently.

The Hypothesis Testing System

- **Monday Morning**: Review past experiments, brainstorm one new hypothesis
- **Tuesday**: Design a test — define metric, timeline, and implementation
- **Wednesday–Friday**: Run the test, collect real-world data

- **Friday Afternoon**: Analyze results, document learnings, iterate

Repeat weekly.

That's not just one good experiment — that's 52 learning cycles per year.

And the best part? Once the system is in place, it doesn't require heroic effort. It becomes rhythm.

🔁 Systems Scale With You

One of the greatest advantages of systems is **scalability**.

As your business grows, your systems grow with it:

- A customer onboarding process can be automated.
- A weekly product review can become a team-wide ritual.
- A content production workflow can involve editors, designers, and publishers.

You don't outgrow a good system — you **amplify it**.

In contrast, goals expire. You hit a target, and you need a new one. Or you miss a goal, and you feel like you failed.

Systems are evergreen. They evolve. They **compound quietly and pay dividends forever**.

📱 Case Study: Aiden, the Solo Founder Who Built a SaaS With Systems

Let's bring this idea to life with a real example.

Meet Aiden.

He's a solo founder who built a productivity app. Instead of setting big, fuzzy goals ("I want 1,000 users"), Aiden focused on three simple systems:

1. Content Creation System

- Every Tuesday, he wrote a blog post on productivity.
- Every Thursday, he shared bite-sized insights on Twitter and LinkedIn.

This built consistent traffic.

2. Customer Feedback System

- After every signup, users received an automatic question:
- "What problem are you trying to solve?"

Aiden collected real-world insights every day.

3. Iteration System

- Every Sunday, he reviewed feedback.
- He made one improvement or bug fix, no matter how small.

This kept the product evolving steadily.

Results after 12 months:

- 12,000 monthly visitors
- 1,800 active users
- 92 paying customers

No viral spike. No big break. Just systems — executed consistently.

🧠 Shift Your Identity: From Goal-Setter to System-Builder

This chapter isn't just about tactics — it's about identity.

A goal-setter thinks: "What should I achieve next?"

A system-builder thinks: "What process can I refine today?"

This mindset shift changes everything.

You stop measuring success by outcomes. You start measuring by **inputs** and **iterations**. You stop chasing. You start building.

Want to become a better entrepreneur?

Build systems for:

- 📈 Learning (e.g., read 1 case study per week)
- 🧪 Testing (e.g., run 1 experiment per sprint)
- 🧠 Thinking (e.g., schedule 1 strategic review every Friday)
- 💬 Customer Insight (e.g., conduct 3 user interviews/month)
- 🛠 Product Improvement (e.g., fix 1 UX issue/week)

Systems turn intention into traction.

✍ Mini Exercise – Build One System Right Now

Let's build a system — right here, right now.

Step 1: Pick a Priority Area

Choose something like:

Marketing

Product development

Hiring

Customer feedback

Onboarding

Step 2: Define the Core Action

What's the smallest repeatable action you could take?

E.g., "Send 5 cold emails/day."

Step 3: Choose the Frequency

Daily? Weekly? Monthly?

Make it predictable.

Step 4: Add a Feedback Loop

How will you track if it's working?

E.g., "Every Friday, check reply rate."

Step 5: Write It Down

System Name: Weekly Outreach

Action: Send 5 cold emails each weekday

Review: Check conversion and reply rate on Friday afternoon

Goal: Refine message weekly, increase conversions by 10% each month

Now put it on your calendar. Make it real. You've just built a system.

💬 Closing Thought: Build Once. Improve Forever.

If goals are dreams, systems are blueprints.

You can't build a house with dreams. But with a blueprint, a hammer, and steady effort, you can create something real — something that lasts.

The scientific entrepreneur doesn't just chase success. They **design** it. They show up whether they feel like it or not. They improve steadily, and they **let systems do the heavy lifting**.

Remember this truth:

> "Don't set a finish line. Design a runway."

When you build the right system, progress becomes inevitable.

Chapter 11: Systems Over Goals — Building Sustainable Success

- How do you differentiate systems thinking from traditional goal setting?
- Can you describe a system you designed that drives consistent outcomes?
- How do you maintain system effectiveness over time?
- How do systems help manage uncertainty in your business?

CHAPTER 12

Feedback is Fuel — Learning from Reality

"If you don't actively seek out feedback, you will eventually get it in the form of failure." — Anonymous Entrepreneurial Wisdom

🧭 Feedback: The Compass of the Scientific Entrepreneur

In science, no discovery is made in isolation. Experiments are designed, results are gathered, and interpretations are revised. One variable changes, and everything can shift. The same principle applies to entrepreneurship.

Every pitch, every landing page, every product launch is an experiment — a hypothesis being tested in the laboratory of the real world.

And the most critical data point from that lab? **Feedback.**

Feedback is not a nuisance. It is not a distraction. It is not a threat. It is the single most valuable input an entrepreneur can receive — a mirror held up by reality.

The scientific entrepreneur does not fear feedback.

They **thrive** on it.

Feedback is how we:

- Diagnose what's broken.

- Confirm what's working.
- Discover what customers actually want.
- Learn how to adjust course with precision and speed.

Ignore it, and your business will drift off course.

Use it, and you'll accelerate toward product-market fit.

But feedback is more than input. **It is the fuel** that powers scientific entrepreneurship. The sharper your ears, the stronger your results.

🔍 Feedback vs. Opinion: Know the Difference

Not all input is useful. In fact, much of what you'll hear as a founder is noise — random opinions masquerading as insights. Learning to filter signal from noise is not just helpful — it's survival.

Here's the key distinction:

Valid Feedback	Empty Opinion
"I didn't understand the onboarding flow"	"It just doesn't feel right"
"The pricing confused me because I thought X was included"	"It's too expensive"
"I expected to see Feature A after clicking Button B"	"This app sucks"

Scientific entrepreneurs know how to **interrogate feedback**:

- Is this coming from a real or ideal customer?
- Is it based on **actual behavior**, not just preference?
- Is it actionable? Specific? Repeated by others?

If the answer is yes, that's data. If not, it's background noise.

> Feedback is only valuable if it's **grounded in experience** and can lead to a change in behavior.

Build this muscle early. It will save you thousands of wasted hours and tens of thousands in development misfires.

🔁 Build Feedback Loops Into Everything

Don't wait for feedback to magically arrive. That's amateur hour. Professional entrepreneurs **design feedback loops** into every layer of their business — so data flows in constantly, systematically, and without friction.

Here are three foundational loops:

🛠 Product Feedback Loop

- In-app micro-surveys (at signup, feature use, or cancellation)
- Usability session tools like Hotjar or FullStory
- Net Promoter Score (NPS) triggers at key lifecycle moments
- Bug report buttons and open-ended feedback forms

These tools reveal what users are **doing**, not just what they say they want.

👨‍💼 Customer Development Loop

- Regular interviews with active and churned users
- Transcripts from support chats, calls, or CRM notes
- Win/loss debriefs from sales calls
- Open-text fields in surveys that ask: "What's missing?"

The goal? Find **patterns**. When three different users say the same thing unprompted — that's a goldmine.

📢 Marketing Feedback Loop

- A/B tests on headlines, CTAs, or email subject lines
- Click-through and bounce rate tracking
- Social media responses and DMs

- Campaign performance comparisons (before/after tweaks)

Your marketing isn't just a megaphone. It's a listening post.

When feedback is embedded into your daily rhythm, you **turn your entire business into a learning machine**.

💥 Why Most Founders Avoid Feedback (And Fail)

Let's be honest — feedback can sting. Especially when it contradicts something you built with love, sweat, and belief.

There are three dangerous founder mindsets that block feedback:

1. Emotional Attachment

> "But we spent six months building this feature!"
>
> Feedback says: "Nobody uses it."

The sunk cost fallacy kills more startups than competition. Scientific entrepreneurs accept reality over ego — even when it hurts.

2. Ego Protection

> "I know what the customer wants. They just don't get it."
>
> This phrase is a death sentence. Your customers **always get it** — because they're the ones who decide whether you survive.

3. Fear of Conflict

> "What if they don't like it?"
>
> Avoiding hard truths won't save you. It only delays the inevitable.

True entrepreneurs ask, even when they're afraid of the answer. And when the answers come, they lean in — because **truth is more important than comfort**.

🧠 Mental Model: Feedback as Fuel

Imagine your startup as a rocket ship. You've built it with care. You've charted a course. You've launched. But in flight, conditions change. Gravity tugs. Wind shifts. Unexpected turbulence hits.

Without feedback, you are flying blind.

With feedback, you adjust course.

With feedback, you make micro-corrections before macro-failures.

With feedback, you can avoid disaster **and** find the optimal trajectory — faster than your competitors.

In other words:

Feedback is not judgment. It is fuel.

📱 Case Study: Pivot by Listening

Amira's AI Startup

Amira, a technical founder, launched an AI-powered writing assistant targeted at students. She had spent months refining her NLP models, perfecting grammar correction, and training her system on academic sources.

Early results were discouraging:

- Low retention
- Low engagement
- Negative reviews

Instead of blaming the users, she got curious.

She reached out to her user base with a simple two-question email:

- "What did you expect this tool to help you with?"
- "What problem were you hoping to solve?"

She conducted 15 follow-up interviews. The insight?

Her assumptions were wrong.

- Most users thought the tool would help write emails, not essays.
- Many were entrepreneurs, freelancers, and professionals — not students.
- They wanted quick, punchy content, not academic perfection.

Amira **pivoted**:

- Repositioned her website and messaging for professionals
- Added templates for emails, social posts, and LinkedIn bios
- Removed academic jargon and emphasized speed

Three months later:

- Retention tripled
- Conversion rate increased 4x
- Revenue doubled

Amira didn't guess. She **listened**.

She didn't pivot randomly. She pivoted with data.

That's the scientific method in action.

🚧 When to Ignore Feedback

Ironically, the more feedback you gather, the more you'll need to **ignore**.

Why?

Because not all feedback is useful. Some is irrelevant, some is misleading, and some comes from users who are not aligned with your vision or audience.

Here's when to **ignore** feedback:

- **The source is outside your target market**

- A feature request from a free user may not matter to your paying customers.
- **The feedback contradicts proven data**
- If 80% of users love Feature A and one user hates it, that's an outlier.
- **The suggestion sacrifices focus for general appeal**
- Not every request needs a "yes." Great products are often defined by what they say **no** to.
- **The feedback reflects untested assumptions**
- Always test. Never assume. The scientific mindset means you treat feedback as **hypothesis material**, not gospel.

🔬 How to Build a Feedback-Driven Startup

Being feedback-driven isn't a one-time tactic. It's a **cultural operating system**. Here's how to embed it:

1. Make Feedback Automatic

- Create triggers for NPS after week 2
- Add in-app surveys after first use
- Send a follow-up email to all churned users asking: "What made you leave?"

2. Respond to Every Signal

- Reply to every message
- Acknowledge all bug reports
- Close the loop when a fix goes live

3. Systematize the Learning

- Weekly team review: "Top 3 feedback insights"
- Track trends in a central dashboard
- Assign an owner to every major theme

4. Use Feedback to Drive Experiments

Every major piece of feedback should lead to one of three responses:

- Test a change
- Reject it (with data)
- Ask more questions

🧠 Case Study: Building with Feedback from Day One

David's Pre-Launch Playbook

David, an aspiring founder with no product yet, started building an AI sales tool. Instead of coding, he spent 30 days talking to 100 potential users.

He asked:

- "What's your current sales workflow?"
- "What frustrates you the most about prospecting?"
- "What would a magic solution do for you?"

He noticed a common theme: writing cold emails was a huge pain.

So instead of building a full CRM, he launched **ColdStart.ai**, a simple tool that wrote personalized cold emails using LinkedIn data.

It wasn't the idea he started with — but it was the idea the market wanted.

By launch week:

- He had 2,000 waitlist signups
- 40% converted to free users
- 10% became paying customers in month one

No product. No assumptions. Just feedback.

🧭 Final Thought: Ask. Listen. Adapt.

Feedback is not a nuisance.

Feedback is not an interruption.

Feedback is **the voice of reality**.

And in entrepreneurship, reality always wins.

If you don't ask for feedback, your competitors will.

If you ignore it, your customers will leave.

If you delay it, your product will decay.

But if you listen — really listen — you'll evolve faster than anyone else.

So ask questions.

Track patterns.

Test what you hear.

Build a company that learns **faster** than the rest.

Because in the end, feedback isn't just fuel.

It's your **unfair advantage**.

> "The fastest learner always wins." — The mantra of the scientific entrepreneur

Chapter 12: Feedback is Fuel — Learning from Reality

- What sources of feedback have been most valuable in your growth?
- How do you filter noise from signal in feedback?
- Can you share a breakthrough that came directly from customer insights?
- How do you embed feedback loops into your everyday processes?

CHAPTER 13

Time as Leverage – Multiplying Results, Not Effort

> *"Give me a lever long enough and a place to stand, and I will move the world." — Archimedes*

🕰️ The Myth of Working Harder

In the early stages of entrepreneurship, hustle is often celebrated. Social media glamorizes the grind — founders working 100-hour weeks, sleeping under their desks, burning the candle at both ends. There's a cultural narrative that if you're not exhausted, you're not doing enough.

But the reality is far less romantic.

Working harder might help you launch, but it won't help you scale. There's a natural limit to how many hours you can work. You can't create more time, but you can create more output — if you understand and apply **leverage**.

Leverage isn't about working more. It's about working smarter. It's the difference between paddling a canoe and building a sailboat. One requires constant effort. The other catches wind and multiplies your movement.

Scientific entrepreneurs reject the hustle culture of diminishing returns. They don't just ask, *"What else can I do?"* They ask, *"What can I design today that works tomorrow — without me?"*

⚖️ What Is Leverage?

In physics, a lever allows a small force to move a heavy object. In business, leverage allows a small effort to create massive results. The formula is simple:

Leverage = Output / Input

High-leverage activities yield disproportionately large outcomes compared to the effort invested. Low-leverage activities — no matter how hard you work — keep you trapped in a loop of effort without scale.

Let's compare two founders:

- **Alex** writes cold emails manually, sending 40 per day.
- **Brianna** uses a cold email automation tool, sending 400 personalized messages per day.

Both work the same 8 hours. But Brianna's results are 10x. That's leverage in action.

Leverage decouples effort from outcomes. It allows you to break the linear relationship between time and value.

🔍 The Four Types of Leverage (Inspired by Naval Ravikant)

Naval Ravikant, entrepreneur and angel investor, famously outlined four types of leverage that modern entrepreneurs can tap into. Understanding these is key to scaling your time and impact.

1. Labor Leverage

Hiring other people to do work on your behalf.

- You trade money for time.
- Great for operational expansion.
- But it scales linearly — more people = more management complexity.

Examples:

- Hiring a virtual assistant to handle emails.
- Contracting developers to build your product.
- Outsourcing content writing or customer support.

2. Capital Leverage

Using money to fund growth.

- Requires access to capital and risk tolerance.
- Used to buy tools, run ads, hire talent, or invest in R&D.

Examples:

- Spending $5,000/month on Facebook ads that return $20,000 in revenue.
- Purchasing scalable infrastructure instead of bootstrapping.

3. Code (or Software) Leverage

Automating tasks with software or code.

- Infinite replication at near-zero marginal cost.
- Works 24/7 without complaint.
- Scales exponentially.

Examples:

- An app that replaces thousands of human tasks.
- An automated onboarding flow that serves thousands of customers.

4. Content Leverage

Creating media that continues to generate value over time.

- No gatekeepers. No limits.
- Builds reputation, drives traffic, generates leads — while you sleep.

Examples:

- A viral YouTube video that sends leads for years.
- A blog post that ranks #1 on Google.
- A podcast interview that attracts investors.

Of these, **content and code are permissionless** — no one needs to "approve" you. You don't need to hire or raise capital. These are the tools of the modern scientific entrepreneur.

🧠 Leverage Thinking: How to Multiply Yourself

Most people are trapped in linear productivity thinking:

1 hour = 1 task

1 task = 1 result

But scientific entrepreneurs build systems:

1 hour = a system that runs forever

1 task = 1,000 results over time

1 meeting = reusable insights for future customers

They constantly ask:

- Can I automate this?
- Can I delegate this?
- Can I record this once and reuse it?
- Can this be turned into content or code?

Example:

Rather than explaining onboarding to every new customer, record a video once. Send it automatically to all new users. That's leverage.

The key isn't just to do more. The key is to **do things that multiply**.

🔄 Compounding Through Leverage

Leverage compounds — just like interest. Each leveraged action unlocks more time, which can be reinvested into even higher-leverage actions.

Here's a typical cascade:

1. You write a blog post →
2. It brings in 1,000 visitors →
3. Visitors sign up to your email list →
4. They get automated emails →
5. They book a sales call or buy directly →
6. The process repeats with no further input

You did the work once, and the system pays dividends indefinitely.

This is how scientific entrepreneurs **escape the treadmill**. Every leveraged move creates momentum that snowballs.

📉 The Hidden Cost of Low-Leverage Work

Founders often feel "productive" when they're busy. But activity isn't the same as progress.

Ask yourself:

- Am I the only person who can do this?
- Will this task matter in a year?
- Am I creating a system or just repeating effort?

Low-leverage work includes:

- Manually replying to every email
- Rebuilding the same slide decks over and over
- Repeating the same explanation to customers
- Managing tasks that could be automated or delegated

These tasks may feel urgent — but they won't build a scalable business.

🛠 Tools for High-Leverage Execution

You don't need to be a tech genius to apply leverage. Here are practical tools that empower any entrepreneur to multiply time:

Automation Tools:

- **Zapier / Make** – Connect apps and trigger workflows automatically.
- **Calendly / SavvyCal** – Eliminate back-and-forth scheduling.
- **Loom / Scribe** – Record walkthroughs or explanations once.
- **Descript / Canva** – Create shareable, scalable content quickly.
- **Notion / Google Docs** – Build centralized systems and templates.

Delegation Tools:

- **Virtual Assistants** – Offload recurring admin tasks.
- **Fiverr / Upwork / Toptal** – Find freelancers for design, development, research, etc.
- **Standard Operating Procedures (SOPs)** – Document repeatable tasks so others can execute them.

Start small. Automate one process. Record one video. Create one piece of content.

🧪 Case Study: Escaping Burnout with Leverage

Talia ran a solo web design agency. Her work was excellent, and clients loved her. But every month was a sprint.

- She spent hours manually crafting proposals.
- Repeated the same onboarding steps every project.
- Was the only point of contact for everything — emails, calls, invoices, revisions.

She hit a wall. More success meant more stress.

So she stopped. She rethought her workflow through the lens of leverage:

- Created modular proposal templates → cut prep time by 80%.
- Recorded onboarding videos → no more repeat calls.
- Used tools to automate scheduling, payments, and file delivery.
- Hired a VA to handle support emails and bookkeeping.

Six months later:

- She worked 30% fewer hours.
- Revenue doubled.
- She launched a course on design systems — a scalable product.

Talia didn't change her industry. She changed her **leverage strategy**.

Multiplying Through Intellectual Leverage

There's another underappreciated form of leverage: **intellectual leverage**.

This is the act of crystallizing your insights into frameworks, strategies, or products that others can use — again and again.

Examples include:

- Turning your process into a downloadable checklist.
- Writing a book or newsletter to share your thinking.
- Creating decision trees or mental models others can apply.

Intellectual leverage builds your reputation, attracts collaborators, and turns your thinking into assets.

🔄 Systems vs. Tasks: The Leverage Equation

Every time you do something manually, ask:

Can this become a system?

Scientific entrepreneurs document and systematize:

- How they make decisions
- How they hire
- How they evaluate experiments
- How they handle onboarding or churn

When you build a company based on systems, your team can operate without constant supervision. Your company becomes a **learning machine**.

💬 Final Thought: Time Doesn't Scale — Leverage Does

You get 24 hours a day. No more, no less.

But scientific entrepreneurs increase the value of every hour. They design for leverage. They think in systems. They build content and code that works while they sleep.

The best founders aren't superhuman. They're **super-leveraged**.

So ask yourself:

- What am I doing that someone (or something) else could do?
- What am I repeating that I could record or automate?
- What am I building that compounds?

Because in the long run, it's not about effort. It's about **engineered impact**.

Don't just work harder. Work multiplied.

⏳ Chapter 13 — Time as Leverage

Choose one:

- Track how you spend your time for 3 days. Highlight your top 3 time-wasters and design a system to reduce them.
- List all recurring tasks. Choose 1 to automate, delegate, or eliminate.

Chapter 13: Time as Leverage — Multiplying Results, Not Effort

- What strategies do you use to multiply your impact without burning out?
- How do you identify activities to delegate or automate?
- Can you describe how compounding efforts helped your success?
- How do you protect time for high-leverage work?

CHAPTER 14

Risk Like a Scientist – Managing Uncertainty Intelligently

"Entrepreneurs don't avoid risk — they design it."

Introduction: Rethinking Risk in Entrepreneurship

Entrepreneurship has long been romanticized as an all-in, leap-of-faith endeavor. You quit your job, pour your savings into an idea, and hope that your vision becomes the next big thing. This perception makes entrepreneurship seem like a roulette table — unpredictable, thrilling, and terrifying. But this depiction ignores the truth embraced by the most successful founders: they are not gamblers. They are scientists of uncertainty.

The scientific entrepreneur does not avoid risk — they engineer it. They understand that risk is not a one-size-fits-all concept but a variable that can be studied, modeled, and managed. Instead of betting the farm, they build a lab. They test, observe, iterate, and refine. From the outside, their actions may appear bold. But from the inside, it's structured — calculated learning with carefully capped downside.

Part 1: Why Entrepreneurship Feels Risky — and Why It Doesn't Have to Be

The Illusion of Chaos

To most people, starting a business means facing an unknown future. You may leave behind a stable paycheck. You may invest your own money or raise from others. You may build something no one asked for. The narrative of entrepreneurship is filled with uncertainty. But the scientific entrepreneur reprograms this view.

The key is recognizing that uncertainty does not equal recklessness. Uncertainty is simply a lack of information — and information can be gathered. Scientific entrepreneurs treat this information gap as a signal to run experiments, not as a cliff to jump off blindly.

Part 2: Redefining Risk — From Threat to Tool

Traditional vs Scientific Definitions

- **Traditional View**: Risk is a threat. It's fear of failure, loss, embarrassment.
- **Scientific View**: Risk = the **possibility** of an unfavorable outcome.

This definition offers neutrality. Risk isn't good or bad. It's a feature of the system. And like any feature, it can be manipulated.

The Three Components of Risk:

1. **Probability** – How likely is an outcome?
2. **Impact** – How significant is that outcome?
3. **Reversibility** – Can the outcome be undone?

Part 3: Risk as a Path to Innovation

Why Scientific Entrepreneurs Embrace Risk

In science, breakthroughs come from the edges — from ideas that might fail. The best scientists don't avoid error; they design experiments that **contain** error. Similarly, innovative entrepreneurs build businesses through trial, failure, and refinement.

Instead of trying to eliminate risk, they make it **safe to fail**.

Part 4: Safe-to-Fail Experiments — The Scientific Approach to Risk

Characteristics of Safe-to-Fail Design:

1. **Cheap** — Minimal investment required.
2. **Reversible** — Easy to pivot or shut down.
3. **Isolated** — Won't infect the rest of the system.
4. **Informative** — Failures yield high-quality data.

Example: Dropbox's MVP

Before building the backend of Dropbox, Drew Houston released a demo video. It simulated the functionality of the product and invited users to sign up for a waitlist. That single video validated massive demand. Houston hadn't risked months of development — just a few days of scripting and editing.

Case Study Callout: Buffer's MVP Email Test

Joel Gascoigne, founder of Buffer, used landing pages and email interest to validate demand before writing a single line of code. With staged pages that progressively asked users to engage, he learned precisely when interest turned into action — for free.

Part 5: Frameworks for Designing Risk

1. Expected Value (EV)

$$EV=(\text{Probability of Success}\times\text{Reward})-(\text{Probability of Failure}\times\text{Cost})$$

EV = (Probability\ of\ Success \times Reward) - (Probability\ of\ Failure \times Cost)

$$EV=(\text{Probability of Success}\times\text{Reward})-(\text{Probability of Failure}\times\text{Cost})$$

Use EV to weigh decisions. If the upside, adjusted for probability, outweighs the downside, it's worth exploring.

Example: Amazon's experiments with AWS began as a calculated risk — but the expected value was massive. The worst-case scenario? Spending resources to develop a tool they could still use internally.

2. Downside Protection

Ask: “If this fails, what’s the worst-case scenario — and can I survive it?”

Techniques include:

- Testing with a limited audience
- Using no-code tools
- Running simulations
- Keeping core resources protected

Case Study: Stripe Atlas

Before Stripe launched its global incorporation tool, it invited a select group of entrepreneurs to test onboarding in a private beta. This allowed for internal feedback loops while preserving Stripe’s brand and minimizing exposure.

3. Reversibility Filter

Ask: “Is this decision reversible?”

- **Reversible** → Move quickly
- **Irreversible** → Slow down, gather more data

This simple filter helps prioritize action and caution intelligently.

Example: Airbnb's Global Expansion

Instead of launching in multiple cities at once, Airbnb tested single-city launches (like Paris) and evaluated local constraints before scaling. This limited the damage of bad assumptions and amplified lessons learned.

4. Pre-Mortems

Imagine the project has failed. Ask: “What went wrong?”

Then work backward to address those potential failure points before they occur.

Tool: Google's "pre-mortem" template is widely used in YC startups and large companies alike.

Part 6: Mindset Shift — From Fear to Feedback

Scientific entrepreneurs see risk not as an emotional burden but as a source of information.

Shift From:

- "What if it fails?"
- To → "What can I learn?"

This reframing builds resilience and clarity under pressure.

Quote: "Every failed experiment eliminates one wrong path and brings me closer to the right one."

Part 7: Deep Case Studies

Case Study 1: SpaceX – Calculated Chaos

Elon Musk poured personal funds into launching reusable rockets. Onlookers saw recklessness. But internally, each mission had strict engineering benchmarks. Failures were expected — even necessary.

By treating each launch as an experiment, SpaceX could afford failure because they used it as input. They recorded massive data on each crash, improving rapidly.

Safe-to-Fail at Scale.

Case Study 2: Amazon – Two-Way Door Decisions

Jeff Bezos popularized the "one-way vs two-way door" mental model. Reversible decisions (two-way) should be made quickly. Irreversible ones (one-way) require data and care.

Amazon Web Services was a two-way door until its success locked in the strategy.

Case Study 3: Airbnb – Regulatory Risk Management

Airbnb didn't tackle legal battles in all cities at once. Instead, they observed, responded, and adjusted to local challenges. This "incremental confrontation" approach allowed them to de-risk by learning jurisdiction-specific nuances.

Case Study 4: Miguel's Pivot

(From earlier example)

Miguel tested a product pivot using a landing page and customer interviews. The cost was nearly zero — and it generated enough data to warrant a product overhaul.

Case Study 5: YC Companies – Test First, Build Later

Y Combinator encourages founders to **test fast, fail fast, and pivot fast**. Most funded startups begin with interviews and spreadsheets, not code. The goal is to de-risk the idea before a single feature is built.

Part 8: Common Risk Traps and Cognitive Biases

1. Sunk Cost Fallacy

"I've spent so much time on this — I can't walk away now."

Solution: Detach emotionally. Data trumps history.

2. Overconfidence Bias

"This idea is so good, it can't fail."

Solution: Build falsifiability into your assumptions.

3. Loss Aversion

"I'd rather avoid losing than try to win."

Solution: Frame learning as gain — even from failure.

Part 9: Practical Risk Design for Founders

Step-by-Step Risk Protocol:

1. **Identify Assumptions**
2. **List Possible Failures**
3. **Run Small Tests**
4. **Use Reversible Moves First**
5. **Measure EV and Downside**
6. **Log Learnings**
7. **Scale Confidently**

Conclusion: Turn Risk Into a Roadmap

Scientific entrepreneurs do not see risk as something to fear. They see it as **raw material** — the essential component of innovation.

By engineering their exposure, designing safe-to-fail experiments, and applying cognitive discipline, they turn chaos into clarity. They learn faster, waste less, and make better decisions — not because they avoid risk, but because they understand it.

"The best founders don't eliminate risk. They design it."

Chapter 14: Risk Like a Scientist — Managing Uncertainty Intelligently

- How do you approach risk assessment systematically?
- What frameworks do you use to mitigate risks?
- Can you share a risk you took that was carefully calculated?
- How do you balance risk-taking with stability?

CHAPTER 15

Building Systems, Not Just Goals

> *"You do not rise to the level of your goals. You fall to the level of your systems." — James Clear*

Introduction: The Great Goal Deception

Every entrepreneur begins with a goal.

"Launch an app in 3 months."

"Get to $10K/month in revenue."

"Build a million-dollar business."

Goals offer direction, but direction is not momentum. Goals tell you where to go, but not how to get there. They can inspire, but they do not create consistency. **Systems**, on the other hand, are the machinery of progress. They are the repeatable processes, feedback loops, and mechanisms that make momentum sustainable and outcomes scalable.

Scientific entrepreneurs don't just dream — they design. They think like engineers, creating processes that predictably produce results. In science, you don't wish for discoveries — you run experiments, analyze the results, and iterate systems. The same logic applies to entrepreneurship.

Section 1: Why Goals Are Not Enough

1.1 Goals Are Temporary

Goals are inherently finite. You either hit them or you don't. If you reach a goal — then what? You're left without direction until a new goal is set. If you miss the goal, it can feel like failure, even if significant progress was made.

For example, if your goal is to reach 10,000 users and you stop after hitting it, what's next? Do you coast, or do you start again from zero? A system, by contrast, continues regardless of milestones — producing users consistently, refining its process with each cycle.

1.2 Goals Without Systems Create Anxiety

When your focus is only on the outcome, the path becomes unclear. You're constantly assessing how far you are from the finish line, rather than improving the way you move toward it. This produces anxiety and reduces performance.

Systems replace that anxiety with process confidence. You're not always measuring distance from a finish line — you're refining your engine to move faster and more efficiently.

1.3 Goals Depend on Willpower; Systems Run on Design

Goals depend on discipline and motivation — both of which are unreliable. Systems reduce the need for willpower because they're structured. You don't decide every day whether to do something — the system decides for you.

This is the difference between forcing outcomes and creating conditions where outcomes become inevitable.

Section 2: What Is a System?

A system is a **repeatable process** that converts inputs into consistent outputs. It has rules, steps, and feedback. In entrepreneurship, systems show up in areas like:

- Lead generation
- Product development
- Hiring and training
- Decision-making
- Customer success

Unlike goals, which are results you *want*, systems are behaviors and processes you *run*. They're built, measured, and improved.

In science, a system is a controlled method for producing knowledge. In business, it's a controlled method for producing value.

Section 3: Systems vs. Goals — A Side-by-Side Look

Aspect	Goals	Systems
Focus	Outcomes	Processes
Duration	Short-term	Ongoing
Motivation	Needs willpower	Needs design
Feedback	Delayed or binary	Continuous
Repeatability	No	Yes
Scalability	Limited	Built-in
Psychological Effect	Stress and pressure	Control and confidence

Goals are useful for direction. But systems are how you **get there** — and stay there.

Section 4: What Makes a Good System?

A well-designed entrepreneurial system has three attributes:

4.1 Clarity

- Each step is clearly defined
- Roles are assigned

- No ambiguity on "what's next"

4.2 Feedback Loops

- The system self-adjusts
- You can measure performance
- You know what to tweak and why

4.3 Scalability

- The system doesn't rely solely on you
- It can be outsourced, automated, or run by others
- It works at 10 customers or 10,000

These attributes make systems resilient, adaptive, and growth-friendly.

Section 5: Feedback Loops in Action

Feedback is the fuel of system design.

Product

- Are users sticking around?
- What features do they use?
- Where do they drop off?

Marketing

- Which channels convert?
- What's your CAC vs. LTV?
- Are messages resonating?

Operations

- Where are delays?
- Which tasks are repetitive?
- What can be automated?

Each feedback loop is an insight generator. Without feedback, systems stagnate. With it, they evolve.

Section 6: Systemization in Practice

Let's translate systems into concrete business areas.

6.1 Lead Generation System

Instead of "I hope leads come in," a system might include:

- A weekly content calendar
- Automated email campaigns
- SEO-optimized blog posts
- Referral loops

6.2 Customer Onboarding System

Instead of onboarding manually each time:

- Use pre-recorded welcome videos
- Automated onboarding emails
- Digital forms and onboarding checklists
- Self-serve help centers

6.3 Product Development System

Instead of building features ad hoc:

- Prioritized feature backlog
- User interviews at regular intervals
- Weekly sprints + retrospectives
- Data-driven iteration cycles

6.4 Decision-Making System

Instead of going by gut:

- Pre-defined criteria (e.g., ROI, risk exposure, urgency)
- Expected value calculations
- Pre-mortem and post-mortem rituals
- Decision journals for learning

Section 7: Case Studies in System Thinking

📌 Case Study 1: Buffer – Scalable Transparency

Buffer famously systematized transparency into their operations. They:

- Made all salaries public
- Created processes for public revenue sharing
- Documented decisions and lessons

This wasn't a PR stunt — it was a system for internal trust and brand differentiation. It made hiring easier, retention stronger, and created viral content — all from a single system.

📌 Case Study 2: Amazon – Mechanisms, Not Mission Statements

Jeff Bezos emphasized "mechanisms" — repeatable processes with feedback. Examples:

- 6-page memos to clarify thinking
- Working backwards from press releases (customer-centric design)
- Weekly metric reviews

These systems replaced cultural fluff with operational excellence. The outcome? Repeatable innovation at scale.

📌 Case Study 3: Anya's Coaching Business

Anya ran a successful coaching practice but felt trapped. She paused to systematize:

- A lead magnet and nurture email system
- Automated onboarding videos and forms
- Course-based delivery instead of 1-on-1
- Content calendar with FAQ repurposing

Result:

- Worked 50% fewer hours
- Revenue grew 70%
- She licensed her system to others

Anya didn't hustle harder — she systemized smarter.

📌 **Case Study 4: SpaceX – Engineering Feedback Loops**

At SpaceX, systems run on iteration:

- Rockets are designed to fail (then learn)
- Every flight logs terabytes of sensor data
- Design feedback cycles occur weekly

This systematic learning has let them achieve what few governments can: reusable rockets at industrial scale.

Section 8: The Mini Framework — I.P.O.F.

Input → Process → Output → Feedback

This universal loop structures any system:

- **Input**: What triggers the system? (e.g., new lead, feature request)
- **Process**: What happens step-by-step?
- **Output**: What's the result?
- **Feedback**: How do we evaluate, improve, or repeat it?

Try applying I.P.O.F. to just one business process. You'll begin to see the power of structured iteration.

Section 9: Systems Create Entrepreneurial Freedom

Most people assume systems are restrictive — the opposite is true.

Systems:

- Reduce decision fatigue
- Automate repetitive tasks
- Create predictable outputs
- Let you delegate with confidence
- Free your mind to think, create, lead

Scientific entrepreneurs build systems so the business runs **without** them — not because they're lazy, but because they understand that creative freedom comes from operational discipline.

Section 10: From Firefighting to Flywheels

Without systems, every day is a fire drill. With systems, each cycle becomes a flywheel — gaining momentum over time.

Flywheels are systems with:

- Self-perpetuating motion
- Compounding impact
- Learning baked in

Amazon's "Prime Flywheel" started with fast shipping, drove customer delight, led to more Prime members, more volume, lower costs, faster shipping — and so on.

What's your business's flywheel? How do you systemize its rotation?

Final Thoughts: Don't Chase Goals — Build the Machine

Ambition is good. Vision is essential. But results come from machines — well-oiled, tested, refined systems.

If you build:

- A system for learning
- A system for marketing

- A system for customer success
- A system for product improvement

Then success becomes a natural output.

“Success isn’t an act. It’s the byproduct of a well-run system.”

Chapter 15: Building Systems, Not Just Goals

- How do you ensure your business systems adapt to changing conditions?
- What’s your process for designing systems that support growth?
- Can you give an example where systems prevented burnout?
- How do systems help you focus on long-term success?

CHAPTER 16

Time is a Scientific Resource – Manage It Like One

> *"Time is what we want most, but what we use worst." — William Penn*

Introduction: The Unforgiving Currency of Time

Every entrepreneur worries about money. That's understandable — money keeps the lights on, funds the product roadmap, and pays the team. But what money takes in visibility, time quietly dominates in impact. Unlike money, time cannot be stored, borrowed, or retrieved. Once it is gone, it is gone — irreversibly. And in the crucible of entrepreneurship, every moment not spent wisely is a moment that could have pushed the business further, tested an idea, or moved one step closer to product-market fit.

Yet, paradoxically, time is often treated with the least intentionality. We waste hours on meetings that don't matter, answering emails that shouldn't have been sent, or tinkering with tasks that bring little return. Why? Because we don't treat time as data. Scientific entrepreneurs do. They quantify time. They test it. They eliminate waste. They make time a variable in their system, not just a background condition.

This chapter is about reengineering your relationship with time — not through hustle glorification or productivity hacks, but by adopting a scientific mindset. You're not just working — you're experimenting with how you work. And that shift changes everything.

Section I: The Scarcity Principle — Time Is the Most Limited Resource

When scientists run experiments, they are constrained — by lab hours, grant deadlines, and peer review cycles. These constraints sharpen their focus. In the same way, scientific entrepreneurs understand that time is their most limiting factor — not capital, not code, not customers. Time is the constraint that defines all others.

Let's be clear:

- **Money can be lost and regained.**
- **Talent can be hired or trained.**
- **Technology can be iterated.**
- **Time? It's the only resource that, once used, is non-recoverable.**

That makes it sacred. And anything sacred demands methodical care.

Scientific entrepreneurs flip the default script. While others ask, *"How much can I get done today?"* they ask, *"What is the best use of this hour to move the business forward?"*

This isn't semantics. It's strategy.

Section II: Thinking Like a Time Scientist

A scientist doesn't just plunge into experiments. They begin by designing the protocol, outlining variables, controlling inputs, and estimating time. They minimize experimental waste and only repeat what produces data. Why should entrepreneurs behave any differently?

Thinking like a time scientist involves three key practices:

1. **Study How You Work:** Observe your habits and identify bottlenecks. Do you procrastinate on hard tasks? Do meetings eat your mornings? This isn't about blame — it's about diagnosis.

2. **Measure Where Time Goes:** Use logs, trackers, or even spreadsheets. Time tracking isn't just about accountability — it's about making the invisible visible. Once you see it, you can change it.
3. **Apply Constraints to Force Focus:** Constraints fuel creativity. When you allocate only two hours to complete a task, your mind discards distractions and locks in. Scarcity breeds precision.

These behaviors shift time from an abstract flow into a manipulatable, testable resource.

Section III: Time as a Testable Hypothesis

Let's reframe how we think about time:

Old Thinking	Scientific Thinking
"I'm busy."	"What am I spending time on — and why?"
"I didn't have time."	"Was this the best use of my attention?"
"I'll try harder tomorrow."	"How can I redesign my workflow to remove friction?"

The point isn't to work more. The point is to work with **more control and clarity**. Like a lab experiment, each day is a hypothesis — and the outcome is your result. If it didn't work, tweak the conditions, don't just repeat blindly.

Ask yourself:

- What hypothesis am I testing with my current schedule?
- What does success look like?
- What would I do differently if I had to justify each time decision with data?

The goal isn't hustle. The goal is validated learning — applied to how you spend your time.

Section IV: Gaining Time Awareness — The First Step

Most people have no clue where their time goes. They think they're busy — but they're just scattered. The cure? Time awareness.

Start with a simple experiment:

1. **Track your time for 3–5 days.**

2. Log every 15–30 minutes. Use tools like Toggl, Clockify, or even pen and paper.
3. **Group activities into buckets:**
   - ● *High-Value (e.g., deep work, sales calls)*
   - ○ *Necessary (e.g., email, basic admin)*
   - ● *Waste (e.g., scrolling, redundant meetings)*
4. **Analyze patterns:**

5. Where is your time leaking? What percentage is spent on value-creating work?

This isn't just introspective — it's transformational. As Peter Drucker famously said:

"What gets measured gets managed."

Section V: Deep Work — The Force Multiplier

Not all hours are equal. One focused hour can outperform five distracted ones. This is the essence of *deep work*, a concept popularized by Cal Newport, who defines it as:

> *"Professional activities performed in a state of distraction-free concentration that push your cognitive capabilities to their limit."*

How scientific entrepreneurs implement deep work.

- Block 2–4 hour periods for high-focus creation. Mornings are ideal.
- Silence all inputs: no email, phone, or Slack. This is your lab time.
- Use tools like the Pomodoro technique: 25 minutes of focus, 5-minute break. Four cycles = 2 hours of flow.
- Batch shallow tasks. Handle emails, quick messages, and admin only during designated periods.

Remember: Your mind is your lab. Protect it like one.

Section VI: Time Economics — Understanding Opportunity Cost

Time is a currency, and every decision is a transaction. That means:

- **Choosing one task inherently means not choosing another.**
- **Every activity has an opportunity cost — the value of what you didn't do.**

Ask constantly:

- ***Is this the highest-leverage use of my time right now?***
- ***Could someone else do this better, faster, or cheaper?***
- ***What if I simply stopped doing this altogether?***

Scientific entrepreneurs audit their calendars ruthlessly. They know that managing time isn't about doing more. It's about doing what matters — and eliminating everything else.

Case Study: Raj's Calendar Overhaul

Raj, a solo SaaS founder, was brilliant but overwhelmed. Working 60–70 hours a week, he was always busy but rarely felt progress.

Step 1: Time Audit

- Product Development: 14 hrs
- Customer Support: 18 hrs
- Meetings: 10 hrs
- Miscellaneous (admin, social): 15 hrs

Step 2: Categorize

- ● High-Impact: Product, Sales
- ○ Necessary: Support
- ● Waste: Social media, reactive emails

Step 3: Redesign

- Mornings: Deep work only
- Afternoons: Calls and admin
- Hired VA for Tier 1 support and email triage
- Canceled low-value meetings

Results After 4 Weeks:

- Hours reduced to 40/week
- Output doubled
- Mental clarity returned

Raj didn't change his ambition. He changed his system. And the results followed.

Section VII: Time Management Frameworks That Work

1. Time Blocking

Assign fixed time slots to tasks — like a scientist allocating lab access. This:

- Boosts focus
- Reduces decision fatigue

- Creates a rhythm of work

2. Eisenhower Matrix

Use this to sort tasks:

	Urgent	Not Urgent
Important	Do Now	Schedule
Not Important	Delegate	Eliminate

This prevents reactive busyness from hijacking your day.

3. Weekly Review

Conduct a Friday review:

- What moved the business forward?
- What was wasted?
- What needs redesigning next week?

This is your *weekly hypothesis test*. Adjust accordingly.

Section VIII: Mental Models for Scientific Time Use

Scientific entrepreneurs don't just manage time — they rewire their beliefs around it. Here are five critical mindset shifts:

"My calendar is my lab."

Every block of time is an experiment. Treat it as such.

"Attention is finite."

Guard your energy like capital. Don't squander it on low-yield distractions.

"Every hour has ROI."

Measure not just how long something takes, but what it yields.

"Distraction is designed."

Your default environment is not neutral — it's engineered to steal attention. Fight back with design.

"Time is a system I can optimize."

Like code or customer funnels, time systems can be debugged and upgraded.

Section IX: Real-World Strategies for Scientific Time Use

📌 Automate Ruthlessly

Use Zapier, Make.com, or native app integrations to eliminate repetitive tasks. A 30-minute automation can save hundreds of hours a year.

📌 Say No — Strategically

Every "yes" to a meeting is a "no" to deep work. Protect your calendar like your life depends on it — because your business does.

📌 Create Thinking Time

Schedule time not just to do — but to think. Insight doesn't come when you're reactive. It comes when you pause, reflect, and connect dots.

📌 Use "Time Debt" as a Red Flag

If you're consistently postponing tasks, that's a signal — either the task is misaligned, over-scoped, or under-resourced. Don't ignore time debt. Investigate it.

Final Thought: Design Time Before It Designs You

Time is always moving. The only question is whether you're directing it — or drifting through it. Scientific entrepreneurs choose to direct. They:

- Measure time like a core metric

- Cut waste with surgical precision
- Design systems that protect and multiply their focus
- Treat time not as a backdrop, but as the key input of value creation

In doing so, they don't just get more done. They **get the right things done** — with clarity, purpose, and leverage.

SIDEBAR BOX: Check Your Progress – Chapter 16

TIME IS A VARIABLE — NOT JUST A RESOURCE

Reflect on What You've Learned

- Am I treating time as a variable I can test and optimize?
- Have I spotted any bloated time cycles in my feedback loops?
- Where has shortening the time-to-insight given me better results?

Apply the Insight

Time-Loop Audit:

Pick one repeated process in your business (e.g., onboarding, product iterations).

→ How long does it take to complete the loop?

→ Where can you compress it to learn faster?

Time-Bound Hypothesis:

Frame a test where time is the key lever:

"What can I release in 3 days that teaches me more than 2 weeks of planning?"

🔁 Time-to-Learning Ratio:

Start tracking how quickly each hour of work yields usable feedback or new insight.

📘 Micro-Tip: Prioritize Learning Speed

Before starting anything, ask:

"What's the minimum time I need to get a useful result from this?"

🔥 Momentum Boost

You've stopped seeing time as a ticking clock—and started using it like a scientist.

You're building time-aware systems.

You're iterating intelligently.

You're learning faster than your competitors.

Keep going.

🔬 Chapter 16 — Time is a Scientific Resource

Choose one:

- Choose a task and deliberately shorten its cycle time (e.g., launch something in 2 days instead of 2 weeks). Reflect on the outcome.
- Calculate your "Time-to-Learning Ratio" for one week. How much time do you spend learning vs. just working?

Chapter 16: Time is a Scientific Resource — Manage It Like One

- How do you treat time as a variable in your experiments?
- What methods help you optimize time usage scientifically?

- Can you share how time management impacted a project's outcome?
- How do you measure the return on time invested?

CHAPTER 17

Emotional Resilience — The Scientist's Mind in the Face of Chaos

"In the middle of difficulty lies opportunity."
— Albert Einstein

Part I: Chaos Is the Constant — Welcome to the Storm

If entrepreneurship had a weather forecast, it would be perpetual storms with occasional sunshine. The skies of startups aren't blue for long. Founders are often sold the dream of independence and exponential growth, but the reality is volatility. Chaos isn't the exception — it's the operating environment.

Imagine this:

- **Customers churn** with no warning after months of product engagement.
- **Product launches** flop after months of build-up and marketing.
- **Investors ghost**, just after promising term sheets.
- **Co-founders fight**, sometimes irreparably.
- **Key hires leave**, burned out or poached.
- **Progress evaporates**, and momentum stalls.

These aren't outliers — they're recurring themes in the entrepreneurial journey.

Yet some founders keep going. Not just enduring, but adapting and growing. They don't deny emotion — they develop **emotional resilience**, not as a platitude, but as a strategic capability.

Resilience Is Not Just Grit

Too often, entrepreneurs equate resilience with raw willpower. They believe enduring hardship without flinching is strength.

But that's not sustainable — and not scientific.

True resilience is not about suppression. It's about **adaptation**.

It's not "grind harder," it's "process faster and smarter."

Scientific Resilience Defined

> **Scientific resilience** is the practiced ability to face chaos with composure, logic, adaptability, and self-awareness — turning emotional turbulence into information.

This isn't about ignoring emotions. It's about developing systems to **observe, interpret, and learn from them** — just like data.

Emotional turbulence can be debilitating. But for the scientific entrepreneur, emotions are **signals**, not stop signs.

Part II: The Emotional Equation — A Scientific Reframe

Scientists deal with failure constantly.

- 90%+ of experiments produce null or negative results.
- Papers are **rejected**.
- Grants fall through.
- Theories are dismantled by new evidence.

And yet science moves forward.

Why?

Because in science, failure isn't personal — it's **informational.**

That same mindset is crucial for entrepreneurs. Let's break down how the emotionally reactive mind differs from the resilient scientific mind:

Emotionally Reactive	Emotionally Resilient
Takes failure personally	Views failure as feedback
Seeks perfection	Seeks iteration
Avoids hard truths	Confronts data directly
Tied to ego and validation	Tied to insight and clarity
Doubts identity	Adjusts strategy

Emotionally resilient entrepreneurs **do not numb themselves**. They cultivate a core belief:

"Emotion is data, not destiny."

Part III: The Lab Mindset Under Pressure

How does a scientist respond when the data disappoints?

With questions.

- "What is this result trying to tell us?"
- "What assumptions were invalid?"
- "What's the next best experiment to run?"

This is the **lab mindset** — detached, curious, and hungry to learn. In the chaos of entrepreneurship, the same mental posture can save not only your startup, but your sanity.

Example: Lab Thinking Applied to Crisis

Your launch flops. Reviews are brutal. Customers request refunds.

You could panic, lash out, withdraw — or you could pause and probe:

- **What is this telling me?**
- **What expectations were misaligned?**
- **What can I test next with lower stakes?**

- **What emotional response is surfacing — and why?**

This mindset isn't natural. But it is **trainable**.

Part IV: Resilience as a Repeatable Feedback Loop

Resilience isn't just a character trait — it's a **process**, like the scientific method. It has a cycle:

1. **Shock** — Something goes wrong.
2. **Pause** — Don't react immediately.
3. **Observe** — What's real vs what's feared?
4. **Reframe** — Formulate a new working theory.
5. **Act** — Take a small, low-risk next step.

Let's walk through this with an example:

> **Scenario:** You lose your largest client. Revenue drops 40%.

- **Shock:** Panic rises.
- **Pause:** You give yourself a day before emailing anyone or posting.
- **Observe:** Was this due to product issues? Budget cuts? Relationships?
- **Reframe:** "If a single client causes 40% collapse, the business is too fragile."
- **Act:** You launch a "diversify revenue" project, and reach out to 5 niche verticals.

This loop is repeatable. With every cycle, you develop resilience **as a skill**, not just an attitude.

Part V: Tools for Building Emotional Clarity

A scientist doesn't rely on willpower alone. They use instruments and protocols. So should entrepreneurs. Here are four of the most powerful resilience-building tools:

1. Pre-Mortem Analysis

Before launching anything major, ask:

> "Assume this fails. Why did it happen?"

List 5–10 hypothetical failure points. Then engineer safeguards.

Example:

- Product bugs? → Add final QA round.
- Weak onboarding? → Pilot test with 5 users.
- Messaging misfire? → A/B test early.
- Misaligned market? → Pre-sell before building.

A calm mind can build clarity. Pre-mortems let you **engineer resilience in advance**.

2. Journaling for Emotional Data

Write down weekly:

- What went well?
- What triggered stress?
- What did I learn?
- What did I avoid?
- What can I control?

This isn't therapy — it's **pattern recognition**. Over time, you'll spot recurring stressors, cognitive distortions, and reactive loops.

Example: You may notice that every Monday after investor meetings, you feel unproductive. That's data. Now you can design recovery rituals post-meeting to prevent downward spirals.

3. The 10–10–10 Rule

Invented by Suzy Welch, the **10–10–10 Rule** is a reframing technique:

> "How will I feel about this in 10 minutes? 10 days?
> 10 months?"

This instantly expands your perspective.

- That angry customer email? In 10 months, you'll forget it.
- That critical tweet? Will it matter in 10 days?
- That funding delay? Could be irrelevant in 10 months if you ship the right pivot now.

4. Recovery Systems

Resilience requires rest. You can't think like a scientist if you're **chronically depleted**.

High performance without recovery is a failure loop.

Design your energy as rigorously as your product:

- **Sleep 8 hours** — Non-negotiable.
- **Move daily** — Walks, weights, yoga.
- **Screen-free time** — Mornings and evenings without devices.
- **No-work zones** — One evening + one weekend day with zero startup talk.

This isn't indulgence. It's **maintenance of the lab equipment — your brain**.

Part VI: Case Study — Sophia and the Spiral

Let's meet Sophia — a founder who learned resilience the hard way.

The Rise

Sophia launched **FocusFrame**, a productivity app for creatives. Her early traction was strong. She raised $500K from angel investors, made TechCrunch, and onboarded 10K users.

Then a major update went live. And broke things.

The Fall

- Bugs corrupted user data.

- Twitter exploded.
- TechCrunch published a scathing takedown.
- Investors went silent.
- Sophia froze. Sleep-deprived, embarrassed, and emotionally drained.

The Rebuild

Instead of quitting, Sophia ran her own post-mortem:

- **Logged the facts** — Customer churn data, NPS scores, app logs.
- **Identified controllables** — Weak testing protocols, rushed timelines.
- **Shut down temporarily** — To sleep, recover, and distance herself from panic.
- **Built again** — Quietly, with no press and a smaller, sharper team.
- **Launched silently** — Let the product speak.

FocusFrame 2.0 now has 50K users — not because Sophia avoided failure, but because she **used it to rewire her process**.

Part VII: Emotional Equations for Entrepreneurs

Let's borrow from algebra — not for numbers, but for clarity.

1. Failure = Data + Emotion

Failure doesn't mean you suck. It means **something didn't work**. Your job is to extract the **data**, discard the **drama**.

Example: If your ad campaign flops, the emotional interpretation might be "I'm bad at marketing." The data says "This message didn't land with this audience."

2. Uncertainty = Opportunity / Ego

The more ego you have — the more you need to be right — the less opportunity you see.

If you drop ego, uncertainty becomes a playground, not a prison.

3. Confidence = Preparation × Evidence

True confidence isn't gut feel. It's earned through preparation and validated through evidence.

Every test you run. Every user you talk to. Every plan you stress-test. That's evidence. That's confidence.

Part VIII: Science Doesn't Panic — It Probes

The scientist doesn't scream at failed results. They **lean in**.

Entrepreneurs can do the same.

> "This isn't a catastrophe. It's a clue."
>
> "This panic isn't prophecy. It's a pattern."
>
> "This is not the end — it's just the start of the next experiment."

Closing Thoughts: The Calm Within the Chaos

Resilience isn't about being stoic 24/7. It's about having **a system for processing storms**.

- You will feel panic.
- You will question your abilities.
- You will hit days where nothing makes sense.

But if you treat those moments like a scientist — with structure, curiosity, and a willingness to iterate — then chaos becomes **context**, not catastrophe.

You are not just the founder.

You are the lab director.

You design not just the product, but the process by which you **rebuild yourself**.

You don't need to feel calm.

You need to stay curious.

That's emotional resilience.

That's the scientific mind — in the eye of the storm.

Chapter 17: Emotional Resilience — The Scientist's Mind in the Face of Chaos

- **How do you maintain calm during periods of uncertainty?**
- **What mental habits help you stay focused under pressure?**
- **Can you describe how you recover from emotional setbacks?**
- **How do you build resilience in your team?**

CHAPTER 18

Feedback Loops — How to Learn Faster Than the Market

> *"Feedback is the breakfast of champions."*
> *— Ken Blanchard*

Introduction: The Fastest Learner Wins

Speed has become the modern entrepreneur's obsession. Everyone talks about first-mover advantage, sprint velocity, rapid launches, and hustle culture. But in reality, the true competitive advantage isn't how fast you build — it's how fast you learn.

Execution is valuable. But *adaptive execution* is unstoppable. In a world of increasing uncertainty, entrepreneurs who can learn, pivot, and adapt in response to reality — not fantasy — will always outpace those who move blindly. You can waste years building something nobody wants. Or you can run tight feedback loops and find truth early.

This chapter is about making feedback your superpower — not by accident, but by design.

Part I: Why Speed of Learning Beats Speed of Execution

The Myth of Execution-First

Silicon Valley often glorifies relentless speed — the startup that launches in 6 weeks, the app that "ships fast and breaks things," the founder who lives in a blur of code and caffeine.

But beneath that mythology lies a graveyard of failed startups that moved fast… in the wrong direction.

Execution without insight is just efficient failure. Building fast is meaningless if you're building the wrong thing. Iterating fast is dangerous if you're iterating off the wrong assumptions. Entrepreneurs don't die from slow code; they die from building in the dark.

Adaptive Speed > Absolute Speed

The fastest runners in business are not those who sprint blindly — they're the ones who recalibrate fastest. They sense change. They process signals. They *adjust*.

This is the heart of scientific entrepreneurship: learning faster than the market moves.

When you move with a tight feedback loop — building, testing, learning, adjusting — you become adaptive. Agile. Antifragile.

Part II: Understanding the Feedback Loop

The Scientific Feedback Loop

In science, feedback is fundamental. Every experiment is a question. The result is an answer — not always the one you wanted, but always data to learn from.

The same is true in business.

The entrepreneurial feedback loop:

1. Build a testable version of an idea
2. Put it in front of real users
3. Collect structured, contextual feedback
4. Identify patterns, not outliers
5. Adjust the product, message, or delivery
6. Repeat

The Power of Iteration

The tighter this loop, the faster your product evolves. You go from assumption to reality, from fantasy to fact. Each loop makes your business smarter.

And if you get this right, you create a compounding learning machine — every action feeds your next insight. You become impossible to ignore.

Case Study: Dropbox's Feedback DNA

In Dropbox's early days, co-founder Drew Houston famously launched a simple explainer video — a mockup — before building the full product. The feedback was instant: users loved the concept. Their mailing list exploded overnight.

Before writing a single line of functional code, Dropbox validated the core user demand. That's feedback-first thinking.

Part III: Separating Signal from Noise

Not All Feedback Is Created Equal

Founders often say, "We're listening to feedback." But *what* they're hearing — and from *whom* — matters enormously.

Useful feedback is:

- Specific and repeatable
- From real or target customers
- Focused on experience, not opinion
- Grounded in behavior, not emotion

Useless feedback is:

- Vague, personal, or reactive
- From non-customers or critics
- Emotionally charged
- Unactionable or inconsistent

Ask yourself:

- "Would 10 more users say the same thing?"
- "Can I build something from this?"
- "Is this feedback about them, or about the product?"

Building Your Signal Filter

To separate signal from noise, establish filters:

- Prioritize feedback from your core use case
- Use structured formats (e.g., survey questions, interview scripts)
- Avoid overreacting to one-off comments
- Focus on themes over time

Over time, your system gets smarter. You stop chasing every opinion, and start hearing the truth.

Part IV: Tools for Scientific Feedback Collection

1. User Interviews — Your Secret Weapon

Nothing replaces one-on-one conversations. A 10-minute user interview can uncover more insight than a thousand analytics events.

Best practices:

- Interview before and after product use
- Ask open-ended, non-leading questions
- Focus on user goals, pain points, and behavior
- Record and tag themes

Sample questions:

- "What were you trying to achieve today?"
- "What did you expect to happen — and what happened instead?"
- "Was anything confusing, frustrating, or surprising?"

- "If this didn't exist, what would you use instead?"

2. In-Product Micro-Surveys

Embed small surveys inside the user experience. Ask:

- "How easy was this step?"
- "What's missing here?"
- "What nearly made you stop?"

This gives you feedback *in context* — the most actionable kind.

3. Analytics: Silent Feedback That Speaks Volumes

Numbers don't lie. Tools like Mixpanel, Amplitude, or GA4 show:

- Where users drop off
- What features are ignored
- What onboarding steps fail
- How time-on-task evolves

Analytics = behavioral truth. Use it to validate or challenge verbal feedback.

4. Feedback Fridays

Block time every week to:

- Read reviews, messages, and complaints
- Log emerging patterns
- Update product backlog
- Reflect on what's working or breaking

This rhythm institutionalizes feedback in your culture.

Part V: Shortening the Learning Cycle

Why Big Experiments Fail Big

Long cycles — six-month projects, full builds, silent launches — are dangerous. You risk building castles on false assumptions.

The solution: tight, fast, cheap experiments.

Think:

- One-hour user tests
- Clickable mockups
- “Wizard of Oz” fakes
- Concierge MVPs
- Unlisted landing pages

These don’t just reduce risk — they multiply insight.

Case Study: Airbnb’s Pre-Launch Experiments

Before Airbnb scaled globally, its founders tested the model locally in San Francisco. They personally took photos of hosts’ homes, talked to users face-to-face, and watched what worked.

That feedback shaped everything — design, messaging, pricing, trust mechanics.

Today, Airbnb runs hundreds of experiments at once. But it started with high-touch feedback loops.

Part VI: Feedback Loop Mistakes and Recovery

Mistake #1: Feedback Comes Too Late

Many founders wait until after launch to gather feedback. By then, it's expensive to change.

Fix: Get user reactions before you build. Pre-sell. Show mockups. Interview early adopters. Tighten the loop at the front end.

Mistake #2: Feedback is Treated as Optional

If feedback is an afterthought, it gets skipped when you’re “busy.” But that’s when you need it most.

Fix: Make it a system. Schedule interviews, auto-trigger surveys, review data weekly.

Mistake #3: Ego Blocks the Signal

Many founders ignore feedback that challenges their vision. That's suicide.

Fix: Kill your darlings. Detach your identity from your features. If it's not helping users win, it's in the way.

Part VII: The Culture of Feedback-Driven Companies

Make Feedback a Company Value

Feedback isn't just a tactic — it's a mindset. Build a culture where:

- Bad news is shared early
- Data wins debates
- Learning beats being right
- Every team member contributes insights

Internal Feedback Loops

Create feedback mechanisms inside your team:

- Regular retrospectives
- Peer reviews
- Anonymous suggestion forms
- Decision post-mortems

A company that learns internally will learn externally faster.

Part VIII: Case Study — Beating Goliath with Feedback

Ravi, a solo founder with two part-time developers, built a tax automation tool for freelancers. His main competitor had raised $40M.

He didn't have ads, capital, or brand recognition. But he had feedback.

What Ravi did:

- Talked to 3 users daily for 30 days
- Removed any feature not used by 5+ testers
- Changed copy weekly based on confusion points
- Shipped based on live chat requests

Meanwhile, the funded giant launched a flashy redesign. It confused users. They churned.

Ravi doubled users in three months. The big company tried to acquire him. He declined.

He didn't win because he was louder. He won because he *listened better*.

Part IX: Feedback as a Habit — Not an Event

Think Like a Scientist Every Day

Adopt the following mindset:

> "Every feature, pitch, email, and process is a hypothesis. Every result is data."

This keeps you out of fantasy. It keeps you grounded in reality. It also creates relentless curiosity — the trait of all great entrepreneurs.

The Feedback Equation

Let's formalize it:

Speed of Learning = Quality of Feedback ÷ Ego

Where:

- *Quality Feedback* = contextual, repeatable, actionable
- *Ego* = your resistance to truth

Want to move faster? Lower your ego. Raise your feedback signal.

Part X: Closing Thought — Become a Feedback Machine

Scientific entrepreneurs don't fear being wrong. They fear learning too slowly.

They don't hide from feedback. They design for it.

They don't seek praise. They seek clarity.

They don't guess. They test.

This is your competitive edge in a noisy world: becoming the fastest learner in the room. Because in entrepreneurship, learning isn't just growth — it's survival.

Chapter 18: Feedback Loops — How to Learn Faster Than the Market

- How do you accelerate learning to stay ahead of competitors?
- What feedback mechanisms give you a competitive edge?
- Can you share how rapid iteration helped you pivot successfully?
- How do you avoid complacency after initial success?

CHAPTER 19.1

The Scientific Pitch — Presenting Ideas with Evidence, Not Ego

> *"In God we trust. All others bring data."*
> *— W. Edwards Deming*

Introduction: Charisma Is Not a Strategy

When we think about powerful startup pitches, our minds often leap to the mythical "charismatic founder." We picture someone with captivating presence, a commanding voice, and a slide deck that dazzles with sleek animations and grand visions. We imagine Silicon Valley rooms falling silent as confident founders declare, "This will change everything."

But charisma fades. Confidence without substance collapses under scrutiny.

What actually wins the confidence of seasoned investors, intelligent customers, and thoughtful partners isn't energy — it's evidence.

The most compelling pitch doesn't shout. It shows.

A scientific pitch replaces ego with clarity, posturing with process, and theatrics with tested truth. It reflects the discipline of a founder who doesn't just believe — but who has measured, tested, learned, and improved.

When you pitch like a scientist, you demonstrate that your idea has already survived pressure. You're not asking for blind faith; you're sharing results. And in the world of high-stakes decision-making, *results speak louder than rhetoric.*

Section I: What Makes a Pitch Convincing?

Most founders assume that pitching is an art form — an act of performance. They rehearse like actors and obsess over aesthetic polish. But while delivery matters, what truly separates weak pitches from strong ones is not charisma. It's credibility.

Credibility is built through discipline, not drama.

A pitch becomes convincing when it has:

- A clearly defined, evidence-backed problem
- A rational hypothesis supported by data
- Actual experimental results — even if early
- A feedback loop demonstrating learning
- A path to scale grounded in traction and iteration

A good pitch doesn't *promise* greatness — it *proves* capability. It doesn't oversell the dream. It shares the evidence that the dream is being built — piece by validated piece.

Let's break this down with a rigorous framework.

Section II: The Scientific Pitch Formula

The scientific pitch follows the same structure used in every experimental process. It's not storytelling *instead* of science — it's science told well.

1. State the Problem Clearly

The strongest pitches begin with a measurable pain point. Not a vague complaint or a hand-waving generalization — a quantifiable, specific friction in the world.

Ask:

> "What exact inefficiency, frustration, or cost is my target customer facing?"

Use data, not drama:

- "34% of small business owners spend over 10 hours/month manually entering receipts."
- "In 2022, freelancers lost $1.3B due to under-tracked expenses."

The goal isn't to evoke sympathy. It's to establish the problem as real, measurable, and worth solving. Numbers ground your pitch in reality.

> Tip: Use third-party studies, surveys, credible public data, or results from your own discovery interviews.

2. Present Your Hypothesis

Once you've stated the problem, show your reasoning — the solution you're testing, not just building.

Structure it like this:

> "We believe that if we build [X], we can reduce [Y] by [Z]%."

This phrasing shows that you're not guessing. You're experimenting.

Example:

> "We believe that a mobile-first, auto-tracking expense app can reduce time spent on tax prep by 70%."

This is clear. It's measurable. It's falsifiable. And it invites discussion rather than defensiveness.

3. Show the Experiment

Now demonstrate that you didn't just *think* about the idea — you *tested* it.

Use real-world validation methods:

- MVPs (Minimum Viable Products)
- No-code prototypes
- Landing page experiments
- A/B tests
- Paid ad traffic tests
- User interviews
- Concierge-style service simulations

🎯 **Example:**

> "We ran a Facebook ad campaign targeting freelance bookkeepers. The ad led to a simple landing page offering a 3-minute demo. Out of 600 visitors, 19% signed up."

This shows you're not in love with your idea — you're in love with discovery.

> ✅ Tip: Include visuals of your MVPs or test flows in your pitch deck to make your experimentation concrete.

4. Reveal the Data

This is where many pitches fall flat. They talk about building something — but don't report what happened.

Your data doesn't need to be perfect. It needs to be honest, relevant, and framed correctly.

🎯 **Examples:**

- "We ran a waitlist test with 500 visitors. 18% signed up."

- "Of those, 54% completed onboarding in under 3 minutes."
- "86% said they'd recommend it to a friend."

This is your "lab results" section. Your results show early signs of demand, usability, retention, or virality.

> ✅ Tip: Always include sample sizes, timeframes, and context. Don't just say "We had 1,000 users." Say: "1,047 sign-ups in 14 days from Reddit and Quora forums, with a 16% activation rate."

5. Explain the Learning Loop

Science isn't just about running tests — it's about learning from them.

Investors and customers want to see how you respond to feedback, refine your assumptions, and adapt your product.

🎯 Example:

> "After interviews revealed confusion during signup, we removed 3 onboarding steps. Completion rates rose 27%."

This shows you aren't just collecting data — you're *thinking with it.*

> ✅ Tip: Include a slide in your deck titled "What We Learned" — it demonstrates humility, insight, and traction in thinking.

6. Present the Vision — with Evidence

Now, finally, zoom out to your vision. But avoid falling into speculative dreaming. Anchor the vision in proof of progress.

🎯 Examples:

- "We grew from 3 to 300 beta users in 8 weeks."
- "Our CAC is $5, with an LTV of $150."
- "We've partnered with 2 major accounting firms."

Avoid empty statements like:

✖ "If we just get 1% of the market..."

✖ "We're going to blow this up once funded."

Instead, say:

☑ "We're seeing 18% week-over-week user growth and are now ready to unlock channel partnerships to expand distribution."

Evidence earns belief. Ego demands it.

Section III: Ego-Based Pitches vs. Scientific Pitches

The Language of Ego-Based Pitches:

- "We just need funding to explode."
- "No one else is doing this."
- "This will be the next big thing."
- "If we get 1% of this billion-dollar market…"

These phrases *sound* bold — but they're red flags. They suggest delusion, not discipline.

Ego-based founders sell dreams. Scientific founders share results.

Section IV: The Investor's Mind Is a Laboratory

Many first-time founders don't realize this, but investors think like skeptical scientists.

When you pitch to a thoughtful investor, they're running internal experiments:

- "Is this founder learning fast?"
- "Are they coachable or defensive?"
- "Do they measure what matters?"
- "Will they pivot if they're wrong?"

A scientific pitch builds the investor's trust because it reflects:

- ☑ Discipline
- ☑ Self-awareness
- ☑ Adaptability
- ☑ Repeatability

Investors don't fund *ideas*. They fund *systems* — and you are the system. Show that you make evidence-based decisions, and they'll believe in your ability to grow through uncertainty.

Section V: Case Study — From Rejected to Funded

Aria, a solo founder, had a powerful idea: a platform to help first-generation college students navigate financial aid. She pitched it passionately to 15 angel investors. The response was consistent:

> "Love your energy, but come back when you've validated the idea."

Rather than take it personally, Aria took it scientifically.

She ran a 3-week experiment:

- Created a landing page with a free downloadable checklist
- Promoted it via student forums and Reddit
- Collected 800 emails and 200 completed surveys
- Identified top needs and confusion points
- Built a prototype and tested engagement

Results:

- 35% weekly active usage
- 12 user testimonials
- 4 letters of intent from university advisors

She returned to the investor pool — no pitch theatrics. Just slides with clean data.

She raised $250K.

Aria didn't become more charismatic.

She became more credible.

Section VI: Tools to Sharpen Your Scientific Pitch

1. Build a "Learning Deck"

Before your formal investor pitch, create a learning deck that shows:

- Hypotheses you tested
- Customer feedback patterns
- Iterations made
- Insights gained

This deck is your *scientific notebook.* It demonstrates not just what you're building — but how you think.

2. Use Metrics with Context

Raw numbers can mislead. Context makes data valuable.

Instead of:

> ✖ "We have 2,000 users."

Say:

> ☑ "We onboarded 2,034 users over 6 weeks via SEO-focused blog content. Our activation rate was 22%, and 8% are daily active."

3. Preempt Doubts with Data

Don't hide your weaknesses. Show that you're tracking them and improving.

🎯 Example:

> "Churn is high among our freemium users. That's why our next sprint focuses on retention —

onboarding nudges, habit loops, and trial-to-paid incentives."

This shows ownership, not insecurity.

Section VII: The Scientific Pitch Mindset

Repeat this to yourself:

"I don't need to impress. I need to demonstrate."

The world doesn't need another flashy founder. It needs more evidence-based builders.

The pitch that survives isn't the one that sounds best — it's the one that works best under scrutiny.

Let your pitch reflect your process. Let your process reflect your thinking. And let your thinking reflect what the world actually needs.

Final Thought

The future doesn't belong to the loudest.

It belongs to the *most relentlessly evidence-driven.*

And that — more than charisma, polish, or funding — is what will make your idea impossible to ignore.

Would you like the placeholder for the diagram included now for this chapter?

Great — here are the callout boxes added to *Chapter 19: The Scientific Pitch — Presenting Ideas with Evidence, Not Ego*, formatted as standalone sections to break up the chapter visually and reinforce key ideas:

🧊 Callout Box: Scientific Pitch vs. Traditional Pitch

Aspect	Traditional Pitch	Scientific Pitch
Problem Framing	Vague and emotional	Clear, data-supported pain points
Assumptions	Asserted as truth	Framed as testable hypotheses
Traction	Vanity metrics (likes, views)	Behavior-based data (activation, retention)
Learning	Rarely discussed	Central to the narrative
Vision	"Revolutionize the world"	Grounded trajectory based on validated insights
Investor Perception	High-risk, unclear thinker	Coachable, disciplined decision-maker

🔬 Callout Box: Quick Checklist for a Scientific Pitch

- ☑ Have I clearly defined the problem with real data?
- ☑ Have I stated my core hypothesis in testable terms?
- ☑ Have I run at least one real experiment?
- ☑ Do I have results with context (timeframe, method)?
- ☑ Can I show how I learned and iterated?
- ☑ Is my vision supported by data, not just belief?

💡 Callout Box: How to Frame a Testable Hypothesis

✖ "We're building a better budgeting app."

✅ "We believe that showing real-time spending alerts will reduce monthly overspending by 25%."

❌ "Our platform helps nonprofits scale."

✅ "We believe a donation optimization engine can increase average gifts by 15% in 30 days."

📊 Callout Box: Use Metrics That Matter

Avoid Vanity Metrics:

- Pageviews
- Social media followers
- Downloads (without activation)

Use Actionable Metrics:

- Activation rate (first successful use)
- Retention rate (week-over-week engagement)
- Conversion rate (free to paid, or visit to sign-up)
- CAC & LTV (if monetized)

🧪 Callout Box: Examples of Simple Startup Experiments

Test Type	Example
Landing Page Test	**"We created a no-code site to measure signup intent."**
Price Sensitivity Test	**"We tested \$9 vs. \$19 plans with a Stripe checkout."**
Retention Loop Test	**"We tested daily vs. weekly reminder emails."**

Onboarding Funnel Test	**"Removed a step to improve first-session completion."**
Copy/Value Prop A/B Test	**"Two taglines — one outperformed 3x in conversions."**

🚀 Callout Box: What Investors Think When They Hear...

What You Say	What They Hear
"If we get just 1% of the market..."	You don't understand segmentation or go-to-market.
"We just need funding to scale."	You haven't validated demand or acquisition cost.
"Nobody else is doing this."	You haven't done a deep competitive analysis.
"We're pre-revenue but about to explode."	You're overly confident with no proof of traction.
"We already have 10,000 users."	Okay, but what's their engagement or monetization?

🧭 Callout Box: Turn Rejection into Scientific Progress

If Investors Say:

"Come back with traction."

Ask Yourself:

- What key assumption haven't I tested?
- Can I run a simple experiment in the next 2 weeks?
- What metric would make this undeniable?

Example Next Steps:

- Launch a waitlist
- Interview 10 users
- Test one core feature in a no-code MVP
- Improve onboarding completion by 20%

Chapter 19.1: The Scientific Pitch — Presenting Ideas with Evidence, Not Ego

- How do you prepare to present data-driven ideas clearly?
- What strategies help you keep ego out of your pitches?
- Can you share how you respond to skeptical questions?
- How do you build credibility quickly with new audiences?

CHAPTER 19.2

The Scientific Pitch — Presenting Ideas with Evidence, Not Ego

> *"In God we trust. All others bring data."*
> *— W. Edwards Deming*

Introduction: The Age of Evidence, Not Eloquence

In boardrooms, accelerator meetings, and investor calls around the world, hopeful founders pitch with dazzling confidence, rehearsed narratives, and high-gloss slides. They lead with vision. They gesture at scale. They quote market size numbers in the trillions.

And yet, more often than not, these pitches fall flat.

Why?

Because what modern investors, partners, and stakeholders seek is not just excitement — they seek **evidence**. They're not buying into a dream. They're evaluating a **hypothesis**. They want to know:

- Has this founder tested their assumptions?
- Do they know their customer?
- Have they validated the problem?
- Are they learning and iterating?

The most compelling pitches today are not ego-driven performances but **scientific presentations of discovery, validation, and traction**. Entrepreneurs who think like scientists pitch like scientists. They don't guess. They don't bluff. They don't sell — **they show**.

This chapter breaks down how to pitch scientifically — with credibility, clarity, and compounding trust.

Section 1: The Power of the Scientific Pitch

A scientific pitch is not a denial of vision — it's a disciplined **pathway to it**. Instead of dramatizing the story, the scientific entrepreneur structures the pitch like a paper:

- **Introduction**: What problem are you studying?
- **Hypothesis**: What do you believe might solve it?
- **Methodology**: How did you test that belief?
- **Results**: What did the data reveal?
- **Conclusion**: What do you plan to do next — and why?

Why It Works

- **Builds Trust Through Transparency:** Investors don't expect perfection — they expect honesty. A scientific pitch communicates what you've tried, what worked, what didn't, and what's next.
- **Demonstrates Competence:** Anyone can say, "We're solving a big problem." A scientific pitch proves it through structured discovery, testing, and iteration.
- **Signals Coachability and Growth:** Founders who test and adapt are founders who learn — a core trait of scalable leadership.

Section 2: The Scientific Pitch Formula

Let's break the pitch down into six foundational parts — a framework to present like a founder-scientist.

Step 1: State the Problem Clearly

> "What major friction or pain point exists in the world?"

The starting point of any compelling pitch is a problem — not just any problem, but a **measurable**, **urgent**, **relevant** one.

Too many founders begin with vague vision statements like:

> "We're revolutionizing wellness."

Instead, anchor the problem in **data**:

> "According to the CDC, 74% of U.S. adults experience chronic stress symptoms weekly, leading to $300B in lost productivity annually."

A strong problem statement does three things:

- Quantifies pain (numbers > adjectives)
- Targets a specific audience
- Indicates urgency or cost of inaction

✳ Example:

> "34% of small business owners spend over 10 hours/month manually entering receipts."

> "In 2022, freelancers lost $1.3B due to under-tracked expenses."

Step 2: Present Your Hypothesis

> "We believe that if we build X, we can reduce Y by Z%."

Every solution should begin as a **testable hypothesis**, not a foregone conclusion.

Ego-based pitch:

> "We built a mobile app to automate expense tracking."

Scientific pitch:

> "We hypothesized that a mobile-first, auto-tracking expense app could reduce time spent on tax prep by 70%."

This subtle shift signals:

- **Humility** (we don't know yet)
- **Intent** (we're trying to find out)
- **Focus** (we are testing one clear outcome)

Step 3: Show the Experiment

> "Here's how we tested our idea."

This is where most pitches lose credibility — when there's no **proof** of real-world interaction.

Avoid generic surveys and focus on real behavior and engagement.

Types of Experiments:

- MVPs — Simplified versions of your solution tested with users
- Landing pages — Used to gauge interest or collect emails
- A/B tests — Compare variations of messaging, pricing, or UX
- Surveys — Targeted and behaviorally-informed (e.g., post-usage)
- Cohort tests — Small group experiments (e.g., 10 users in a pilot)

✳ **Example:**

> "We launched a Typeform landing page with a 2-minute demo video. Out of 500 viewers, 120 signed up (24% CTR), and 78 completed onboarding (65%)."

This isn't fluff — it's **lab data**.

Step 4: Reveal the Data

"Here's what happened."

This is your **results** moment. Clean, clear metrics are your currency. Investors aren't looking for big numbers — they're looking for **signal**.

Good metrics share:

- Sample size
- Timeframe
- Conversion rates
- Retention indicators
- Behavior, not opinion

Bad metrics include:

- Vanity stats (e.g., total downloads without usage)
- No context (e.g., "We have 1,000 users" — but how active?)

✳ Example:

> "We had 1,000 site visits over 10 days. 23% clicked 'Get Started.' Of those, 72% completed sign-up, and 41% returned a second time within 48 hours."

Even a small dataset, when cleanly presented, can drive belief.

Step 5: Explain the Learning Loop

"Here's how we adapted based on feedback."

You didn't just test — **you learned**.

Show:

- What users struggled with
- What you changed
- What impact it had

✷ Example:

> "We removed 3 onboarding steps after interviews revealed confusion. Completion rates rose 27%."

This shows agility, responsiveness, and user-centricity.

Step 6: Present the Vision — Backed by Evidence

> "Now that we know this works, here's how we scale it."

You've proven your concept in micro. Now zoom out — but stay **data-driven**.

Weak:

> "We'll dominate the market once we raise funding."

Strong:

> "We've gone from 3 to 300 users in 8 weeks, maintained a 61% weekly retention rate, and have a CAC of $5 with an LTV of $150."

Add signals of validation:

- Partnerships
- Repeat usage
- User testimonials
- Revenue growth
- Waitlists

Section 3: The Dangerous Allure of Ego-Based Pitching

Ego-based pitching is seductive — it's fast, loud, and dramatic. But it backfires.

Common Signs:

- "We just need funding to blow it up."

- "This is the next big thing."
- "No one else is doing this."
- "If we get 1% of the market…"

These phrases reek of **assumption**, not **validation**.

They communicate:

- Overconfidence
- Shallow research
- Lack of testing
- Magical thinking

Investors know the odds. They're not looking for bluster — they're looking for builders.

Section 4: Inside the Investor's Mind

Most investors operate with a **scientific lens**:

- Is this founder learning fast?
- Do they think in experiments?
- Are their insights earned, not assumed?
- Can I trust how they process feedback?

What wins is not charisma — it's clarity, iteration, and traction.

The scientific pitch answers the three burning questions every investor silently asks:

1. Do they understand the problem deeply?
2. Are they capable of learning and adapting?
3. Can they execute repeatably?

Section 5: Case Study — From Rejected to Funded

Meet Aria, a solo founder building a tool for nonprofits to streamline donor communication.

First Pitch:

- Passionate, articulate, driven
- Beautiful slides, strong story
- But: no data, no traction, no users

Investor response:

"We love your passion. Come back with validation."

Aria's Response (90 Days):

- Launched a free prototype on Carrd
- Ran Reddit ads for $200
- Got 800 signups, with 200 active testers
- Conducted 30 user interviews
- Tracked cohort usage weekly

Second Pitch:

- Quiet, calm, confident
- Data-rich:
- "35% weekly active usage"
- "12 repeat customer stories"
- "4 pilot partnerships underway"

Result:

She raised **$250K** from two firms.

She didn't become more charismatic.

She became more **scientific**.

Conclusion: Pitching as an Ongoing Experiment

The best pitches aren't performances. They're **presentations of discovery**. A scientific pitch is not a marketing tool — it's a **trust-building process** rooted in clarity, humility, and truth.

Don't raise money with vision alone.

Raise it with **evidence**.

Don't chase applause.

Chase **accuracy**.

Because in entrepreneurship, as in science, the most credible voice in the room isn't the loudest — it's the one with the **most validated learning**.

🎤 Chapter 19 — The Scientific Pitch

Choose one:

- Rewrite your pitch using the structure: Hypothesis → Evidence → Outcome → Ask.
- Record yourself giving your pitch. Watch it back and note 3 places where you could replace fluff with data.

Chapter 19.2: The Scientific Pitch — Mastering Strategic Storytelling

- How do you craft stories that balance ambition and evidence?
- What techniques help make complex ideas accessible?
- Can you describe how narrative helped you win support?
- How do you tailor your story to different stakeholders?

CHAPTER 20

The Endless Experiment — Embracing the Journey Beyond Success

The Myth of the Final Destination

Success is often portrayed as a finish line — a grand exit, a market conquest, or a celebrated IPO. But for the scientific entrepreneur, success is never final. It is a milestone, not a conclusion. True entrepreneurship, like science, is an endless process of exploration, refinement, and discovery. Each breakthrough opens new questions. Each solved problem unveils a more complex challenge. And each "win" — whether a product-market fit or a profitable quarter — merely sets the stage for the next experiment.

The scientific entrepreneur embraces this truth: the journey never ends, because progress never ends. In this final chapter, we go beyond the metrics, the frameworks, and the playbooks to explore the mindset that sustains lifelong innovation — a commitment to endless curiosity, continuous iteration, and evolving purpose.

Redefining What "Success" Means

In the traditional narrative, success is about arrival — reaching a specific goal: funding, revenue, acquisition, influence. But for the scientific entrepreneur, success is a function of:

- **Learning velocity**: How quickly are you gaining useful, testable knowledge?

- **Positive impact**: How does your venture improve lives, systems, or futures?
- **Adaptability**: Are you becoming more resilient, flexible, and open-minded over time?
- **Personal alignment**: Does your work increasingly reflect your values and strengths?

This reframing changes the game. You're no longer chasing external validation or static outcomes. You're playing an infinite game of learning, where each iteration is meaningful in itself — not just as a means to an end.

Infinite Games vs. Finite Goals

James Carse, in his seminal work *Finite and Infinite Games*, defines two kinds of games: finite games are played for the purpose of winning, while infinite games are played for the purpose of continuing the play.

Most entrepreneurs, especially early on, treat business like a finite game — reach $1M ARR, raise a Series B, dominate the category. But scientific entrepreneurs learn to treat it as an infinite game. They ask:

- How do I build a business that keeps evolving?
- How do I create systems that keep learning?
- How do I contribute to a mission that outlasts me?

By adopting the mindset of infinite play, you remain open to possibility, unafraid of pivoting, and unbound by any single definition of victory. You realize that the point is not to win — the point is to keep growing.

The Second Mountain: From Achievement to Contribution

David Brooks, in *The Second Mountain*, describes two phases of life. The first mountain is about achievement — building, proving, acquiring. But after climbing it, many find it hollow. They then begin the second climb — one of service, meaning, and deeper fulfillment.

Scientific entrepreneurs often undergo this transition. After initial "success," they start asking:

- What am I really here to build?
- Who am I doing this for?
- What's the highest use of my time and talents now?

This transition is not about retreating from ambition. It's about **evolving** ambition — from ego-driven goals to purpose-driven experiments. The scientist doesn't stop researching after a breakthrough. They go deeper. The entrepreneur doesn't retire after an exit. They re-enter with greater clarity.

Case Study: Stewart Butterfield (Slack, Flickr)

Stewart Butterfield's journey is a prime example of the endless experiment. His team originally set out to build a game called *Glitch*, which failed commercially. But in the process, they developed an internal communication tool — Slack. That pivot led to one of the fastest-growing B2B software products in history.

After Slack's success, Butterfield could have walked away. But instead, he stayed curious. He invested time in making work communication more humane, team-centric, and joyful. His leadership wasn't about chasing "the next big thing." It was about deepening an experiment already in motion: improving how people collaborate.

His mindset reflects the scientific entrepreneur's ethos: failure is data, success is a platform, and the process itself is the prize.

The Role of Curiosity and Humility

At the core of endless experimentation lies two fundamental traits:

1. **Curiosity** — the drive to explore beyond the known

2. **Humility** — the willingness to be wrong and still move forward

Scientific entrepreneurs know that certainty is an illusion. What works today may not work tomorrow. What you believe now might be outdated next year. So they remain curious — not only about markets and products, but about themselves.

They ask:

- What am I assuming here?
- Where might I be wrong?
- What haven't I tried yet?

This self-questioning loop is what keeps innovation alive. Ego seeks affirmation; curiosity seeks truth. And truth — however uncomfortable — always leads to better results.

Long-Term Thinking in a Short-Term World

We live in a world obsessed with speed: fast growth, fast exits, fast fame. But science — and real entrepreneurship — unfolds over long timelines. The greatest ventures are often decades in the making. Think of:

- Amazon, which didn't post meaningful profits for years
- Tesla, which faced near-bankruptcy multiple times before mass adoption
- SpaceX, which risked everything on one final rocket launch

What sustained these founders wasn't just vision. It was long-term commitment to a set of experiments. They weren't gambling on outcomes. They were refining systems, building infrastructure, and testing hypotheses at scale.

Scientific entrepreneurs must resist the trap of short-termism. They build for decades, not quarters. They optimize for resilience, not vanity. They pursue wisdom, not headlines.

Legacy Is an Emergent Property

You don't get to dictate your legacy — it emerges from consistent patterns of action. The entrepreneurs we remember most aren't the ones who shouted the loudest. They're the ones who stayed in the lab, stayed on the path, and kept evolving with integrity.

Legacy is not something you build for. It's something you build **through** — through how you treat your team, how you handle failure, how you make decisions under uncertainty, and how you show up when nobody's watching.

The scientific entrepreneur understands: the real reward is becoming someone worth remembering — not because you won, but because you never stopped learning.

The Final Mindset Shift: From Builder to Steward

In the early stages, you are the builder — the one who tests, iterates, and drives momentum. But as your venture matures, your role must evolve. You become a **steward** — of culture, of purpose, of the next generation.

Stewardship means asking:

- How do I make sure this system can survive without me?
- How do I pass on what I've learned to others?
- How do I protect the integrity of the mission as it scales?

The steward thinks beyond themselves. They cultivate leaders. They systematize wisdom. They build institutions that can withstand the entropy of time.

And in doing so, they fulfill the highest calling of the scientific entrepreneur: to leave the world not just better, but better equipped to keep improving.

Chapter 20: The Endless Experiment — Embracing the Journey Beyond Success

- How do you stay motivated when there's no final destination?
- What habits support continuous adaptation and learning?
- Can you share how embracing uncertainty shaped your growth?
- How do you keep experimenting when things are going well?

The Journey Continues

You've now explored the full arc of the scientific entrepreneur — from identifying problems, designing experiments, learning from failure, managing risk, building systems, and measuring what matters, all the way to navigating success with humility and embracing the journey beyond it.

This chapter is the final one in this book, but not in your journey. In fact, it's only a preface — a call to begin again, with fresh eyes and deeper insight.

Because the work isn't done. The future is still unknown. And the next experiment is waiting.

So go — with curiosity as your compass, evidence as your map, and purpose as your engine. The world needs more scientific entrepreneurs. And now, you are one of them.

Here's to your journey.

Here's to the endless experiment.

— **Arham Amit Lalgunkar**

✅ **Tag your progress with #ScientificEntrepreneur or DM @arham.lalgunkar on Instagram. Let me know what you're testing.**

This is your lab now. Make it count.

About the Author

I'm Arham Amit Lalgunkar — a researcher, systems thinker, and lifelong learner deeply curious about how businesses work, why they fail, and how they succeed through evidence, discipline, and innovation.

Though I haven't yet built a startup of my own, my passion for entrepreneurship has driven me to study it relentlessly. I've spent years reading, observing, analyzing, and synthesizing ideas from the world's best business minds. From **Grade 8 to the beginning of Grade 11**, I researched and wrote what would become this book. I took a short pause during **Grade 10** to focus on exams, but the vision never left me.

This book, ***The Scientific Entrepreneur***, is the result of that journey — a **compilation of the research I've done over several years**. I explored **hundreds of YouTube videos**, **business articles**, **financial newspapers**, and **social media platforms** where people generously share their knowledge about entrepreneurship and money-making strategies.

Special thanks to the countless **YouTubers**, **bloggers**, and creators across platforms like **Reddit**, **Quora**, **Medium**, **Twitter/X**, and **LinkedIn**, who post in-depth insights, real-life stories, and practical advice for aspiring entrepreneurs. You've been my digital mentors and your content laid the foundation for many of the ideas in this book.

I'm especially grateful to **JSS Private School, Dubai**, for fostering my growth and supporting my journey. A heartfelt thank you to our **Principal, Ms. Chitra Sharma**, our **Vice Principal, Ms. Bindhu**

Rajiv, and our **CEO, Mr. Govindrao Naik** for believing in student voices and giving us room to dream big. I also owe immense thanks to all my **teachers**, whose guidance inside and outside the classroom shaped the way I think and work.

Above all, my deepest gratitude goes to my **parents**. Your constant support, encouragement, and belief in me gave me the strength to keep writing—even when it was difficult. This book wouldn't exist without your love.

The Scientific Entrepreneur isn't a manual of shortcuts or a collection of overnight success stories. It's a mindset guide — born from real research, personal reflection, and years of curiosity. If I could write this book between the ages of **12 and 16**, I hope it reminds you that age is not a barrier to thinking deeply, learning continuously, and sharing your voice with the world.

Outside of research and writing, I enjoy structured thinking, creative problem-solving, and helping others test and bring their boldest ideas to life.

Here's to your experiments, your growth, and your journey ahead.

— Arham Amit Lalgunkar

If you'd like to connect, share your thoughts, or just say hello, feel free to reach out:

arhamlalgunkar@gmail.com

Instagram:

ARHAM.LALGUNKAR

Thank you for reading — and good luck on your own path to becoming a scientific thinker and builder.

💥 The $10K Playbook

Your First Scientific Venture

"Don't just read. Build. Don't just hope. Test."

If you've read this far, you're already different. You're a thinker. A builder. A scientist of possibility. This page is your invitation to take action — with a simple business model designed to help you earn your first $5,000–$10,000, fast.

You don't need funding. You don't need luck. You need execution, feedback, and focus.

🔁 The Micro-Service Agency Model

🎯 Step 1: Choose a Niche Skill

Start with something you know or can learn quickly.

Examples:

- Notion dashboards for solopreneurs
- AI prompt creation for businesses
- Instagram automation for coaches
- Newsletter strategy for creators
- Landing page design for startups

Tip: Focus on *painkiller* skills, not just nice-to-haves.

📦 Step 2: Productize It

Turn your skill into a clear, repeatable package.

Example:

> "I'll build your automated Notion workspace in 72 hours – $500 flat."

Keep it simple. Clear value. Fast turnaround. No custom work.

🌐 Step 3: Build a 1-Page Website

Use Carrd, Notion, or Framer. Include:

- Headline ("Done-for-you AI Landing Pages")
- What you offer, for whom, and how much
- A button to book or DM you

Don't overthink the design — clarity wins.

💎 Step 4: Get Your First 5 Clients

Use:

- Cold DMs on X (Twitter), IndieHackers, LinkedIn
- Share before/after work samples
- Offer your first 2–3 at a discount in exchange for testimonials

> "Hey, I help creators set up AI newsletters. Want a free setup in exchange for a case study?"

⚙️ Step 5: Systematize & Scale

Once you've served 3–5 clients:

- Turn delivery into a checklist
- Automate tasks with Zapier, Make, Airtable
- Hire help to grow via Upwork or Fiverr

💡 Bonus: Recurring Revenue

Once clients trust you, upsell:

- Monthly updates
- Optimization
- Strategy sessions
- Simple services, high margin.

🚀 Your Challenge

Launch this within **7 days of finishing the book.**

Track your results. Tweak your pitch. Keep learning.

This *is* your first experiment — and it just might change everything.

Proof over promises. Start today. Grow forever.

Research Sources & Acknowledgments

This research sources & acknowledges the foundational thinkers, researchers, entrepreneurs, publications, platforms, and media referenced or drawn upon throughout *The Scientific Entrepreneur*. Each chapter integrates insights from a wide array of credible, time-tested, and field-tested materials. Below are the key sources, categorized and cross-linked to the corresponding chapters.

Books, Authors, and Thought Leaders

- Eric Ries – *The Lean Startup* → Chapter 5: Lean experimentation, MVPs
- Steve Blank – *The Startup Owner's Manual* → Chapters 5, 8, 10: Customer discovery, hypothesis validation
- Clayton Christensen – *The Innovator's Dilemma* → Chapters 3, 6: Disruptive innovation, scientific iteration
- Jim Collins – *Good to Great* → Chapters 2, 13: Level 5 leadership, systems thinking
- Nassim Nicholas Taleb – *Antifragile*, *The Black Swan* → Chapters 4, 14: Risk, randomness, uncertainty
- Daniel Kahneman – *Thinking, Fast and Slow* → Chapter 14: Cognitive bias, decision-making
- Peter Thiel – *Zero to One* → Chapters 2, 3: Vertical progress, original thought
- Charles Duhigg – *The Power of Habit* → Chapter 15: Systems and behavioral design
- James Clear – *Atomic Habits* → Chapter 15: System-building, habits vs. goals

- Naval Ravikant – Podcast appearances, Twitter essays → Chapter 13: Time leverage, automation
- Marc Andreessen – *The Only Thing That Matters* (Blog post) → Chapter 9: Product/market fit
- Andrew Chen – *The Cold Start Problem* → Chapter 7: Network effects, scaling metrics
- Ben Horowitz – *The Hard Thing About Hard Things* → Chapters 1, 16: Founder challenges, organizational systems
- Paul Graham – Y Combinator Essays → Chapters 5, 10, 12: Experimentation, founder advice
- Simon Sinek – *Start with Why* → Chapter 1: Purpose-driven entrepreneurship
- Carol Dweck – *Mindset* → Chapter 2: Growth mindset in scientific thinking
- Scott Adams – How to Fail at Almost Everything and Still Win Big → Chapter 15: Systems over goals

Academic Papers and Research

- Harvard Business Review articles on metrics, culture, and innovation → Chapters 7, 11, 12
- MIT Sloan Management Review – *Using Data to Drive Strategy* → Chapter 7
- Journal of Business Venturing – Research on lean startup and entrepreneurial learning → Chapters 5, 8
- Stanford eCorner Lectures and Case Studies → Chapters 3, 6, 9
- McKinsey & Co. – *The Business Value of Design* → Chapter 9: Product innovation
- London Business School – Research on entrepreneurial uncertainty → Chapter 14
- Kellogg School of Management – Feedback loops in organizational design → Chapter 15

YouTube & Podcast References

- Y Combinator Startup School – Eric Migicovsky, Michael Seibel → Chapters 5, 6, 10
- Stanford eCorner Talks – Reid Hoffman, Daphne Koller, Marissa Mayer → Chapters 3, 4, 6
- Lex Fridman Podcast – Naval Ravikant, Balaji Srinivasan → Chapters 13, 14
- How I Built This (NPR) – Founders from Airbnb, Dropbox, Stripe, Patagonia → Chapters 7, 9, 16
- Masters of Scale – Reid Hoffman interviewing tech leaders → Chapters 5, 12, 14
- Tim Ferriss Podcast – Deep dives with startup builders, authors → Chapters 1, 13, 15
- The Knowledge Project – Shane Parrish interviews on mental models, systems → Chapters 13, 15
- The Indie Hackers Podcast – Real-life founder experiments and pivots → Chapters 5, 8, 11

Websites and Blogs

- First Round Review → Chapter 10: Early-stage growth, hiring systems
- Andreessen Horowitz Blog → Chapter 9: Go-to-market, product design, startup frameworks
- Paul Graham Essays → Chapter 3: Idea selection, Chapter 12: Feedback
- Naval Ravikant's Almanack → Chapter 13: Leverage, wealth creation
- Farnam Street – Mental models, systems, decision-making → Chapters 13, 15
- Lenny's Newsletter – Product growth advice → Chapters 6, 7, 9
- Wait But Why – Longform thinking → Chapter 2: First principles

- CB Insights Research → Chapter 4: Why startups fail
- Stripe Press – Entrepreneurial essays and deep research → Chapter 3
- Product Hunt → Chapter 6: Early traction, feedback loops

News and Media Outlets

- TechCrunch – Startup launches, failures, pivots → Chapter 4
- Forbes – Entrepreneurial metrics and funding reports → Chapters 7, 8, 9
- The Information – In-depth startup news → Chapters 6, 7
- Bloomberg Businessweek – Startup market disruptions → Chapters 3, 9
- Fast Company – Culture, innovation, systems → Chapters 10, 15
- Wired – Emerging tech and disruption stories → Chapters 3, 6, 14
- The Economist – Data-driven strategy, macro trends → Chapter 13

LinkedIn Thought Leaders & Articles

- Andrew Chen (a16z) – Network effects, cold start → Chapter 7
- Julie Zhuo – Product design and leadership → Chapter 9
- Brian Balfour – Growth loops, metrics → Chapters 7, 10
- Shreyas Doshi – Product thinking, strategy → Chapter 9
- Casey Winters – Marketplace growth advice → Chapters 6, 7
- Kunal Shah – Philosophy of scale, Indian startup insights → Chapter 14

Selected Tools and Models Referenced

- OKRs (John Doerr) → Chapter 10

- Lean Canvas – Ash Maurya → Chapter 5
- Net Promoter Score (NPS) → Chapter 7
- Pirate Metrics (AARRR framework) → Chapter 7
- Eisenhower Matrix → Chapter 13: Time prioritization
- Systems Thinking (Peter Senge) → Chapter 15
- Cynefin Framework → Chapter 14: Managing complexity
- Toyota Production System / Kaizen → Chapter 8: Experimentation

Additional Acknowledgments

- Thousands of hours of startup interviews, podcast transcripts, open-source founder decks, YC demo days, GitHub README files, Substack newsletters, and academic courses contributed to this work.
- Many insights were synthesized through long-term observation of emerging companies, failures, and live experimentation during real startup development.

This research sources & acknowledges is a living document. If you believe your content has been meaningfully referenced without appropriate credit, please contact me. This book exists, thanks to the cumulative work of countless thinkers who share knowledge generously with the world.

NOTES